W9-BFM-390

DATE DUE

MAY 8			
JUN 6 '85			

The Renaissance

Other books in the History Firsthand series:

HISTORY
FIRSTHAND

The Renaissance

Raymond Obstfeld and Loretta Obstfeld,
Book Editors

Daniel Leone, *President*
Bonnie Szumski, *Publisher*
Scott Barbour, *Managing Editor*
David M. Haugen, *Series Editor*

GREENHAVEN PRESS
SAN DIEGO, CALIFORNIA

THOMSON
★
GALE

Detroit • New York • San Diego • San Francisco
Boston • New Haven, Conn. • Waterville, Maine
London • Munich

Library of Congress Cataloging-in-Publication Data

The Renaissance / Raymond Obstfeld, Loretta Obstfeld, book editors.
        p.   cm. — (History firsthand)
    Includes bibliographical references and index.
    ISBN 0-7377-1079-9 (pbk. : alk. paper) —
    ISBN 0-7377-1080-2 (lib. bdg. : alk. paper)
    1. Renaissance. I. Obstfeld, Raymond, 1952– . II. Obstfeld,
Loretta. III. Series.

CB361 .R372   2002
940.2'1—dc21   2001051296

Cover photo: © Wood River Gallery
Library of Congress, 25, 27, 65, 77, 121, 130
North Wind Picture Archives, 55
© Wood River Gallery, 22

Printed in the USA

Contents

Chapter 1: A New Age of Humanism

1. On the Dignity of Man
Pico argues against the medieval belief that human
spiritual progress is predestined. On the contrary,
he states that humans are free to determine their
own place in the world according to their self-
determination and individual nature.

2. A Complaint of Peace
The Middle Ages was marked by numerous religious
wars, social injustice against lower classes, and other
disharmony. Erasmus decries such miseries and
makes a plea for a new age that embraces universal
peace and justice.

3. The Excellence of This Age
The numerous accomplishments of the Renaissance
era are surveyed in order to demonstrate that it was a
golden age spanning many countries and many disciplines, not the achievement of any one people. All the
advancements reflect the kind of thinking, artistic,
and moral people that God favors upon the Earth.

4. The Advancement of Learning
Fearing that society is too strictly bound by traditional ways of looking at the world, English scientist
Bacon proposes a new system for learning that emphasizes reason over tradition, and encourages individuals to seek truth no matter where it leads or what
impact it has on conventional beliefs.

Renaissance Man is presented as an allegory for overcoming obstacles in order to achieve a higher spirituality. This sense of personal searching for understanding and fulfillment expresses a new direction in philosophy that will come to characterize the Renaissance.

importance of people observing the world for themselves, rather than merely accepting the way others before them have understood the world. Extolling the virtues of the eye over other organs, he explains how art is a precise science of observation and recording rather than mere whimsical interpretation.

Chapter 6: Daily Life

count of a witch trial details the seriousness of accusations of witchcraft, a crime punishable by death.

4. The Great Fire of London
In one of the most famous diaries in history, politician and statesman Pepys describes the disastrous Great Fire that destroyed most of the city of London on September 2, 1666.

Foreword

In his preface to a book on the events leading to the Civil War, Stephen B. Oates, the historian and biographer of Abraham Lincoln, John Brown, and other noteworthy American historical figures, explained the difficulty of writing history in the traditional third-person voice of the biographer and historian. "The trouble, I realized, was the detached third-person voice," wrote Oates. "It seemed to wring all the life out of my characters and the antebellum era." Indeed, how can a historian, even one as prominent as Oates, compete with the eloquent voices of Daniel Webster, Abraham Lincoln, Harriet Beecher Stowe, Frederick Douglass, and Robert E. Lee?

Oates's comment notwithstanding, every student of history, professional and amateur alike, can name a score of excellent accounts written in the traditional third-person voice of the historian that bring to life an event or an era and the people who lived through it. In *Battle Cry of Freedom*, James M. McPherson vividly re-creates the American Civil War. Barbara Tuchman's *The Guns of August* captures in sharp detail the tensions in Europe that led to the outbreak of World War I. Taylor Branch's *Parting the Waters* provides a detailed and dramatic account of the American Civil Rights Movement. The study of history would be impossible without such guiding texts.

Nonetheless, Oates's comment makes a compelling point. Often the most convincing tellers of history are those who lived through the event, the eyewitnesses who recorded their firsthand experiences in autobiographies, speeches, memoirs, journals, and letters. The Greenhaven Press History Firsthand series presents history through the words of first-person narrators. Each text in this series captures a significant historical era or event—the American Civil War, the

Great Depression, the Holocaust, the Roaring Twenties, the 1960s, the Vietnam War. Readers will investigate these historical eras and events by examining primary-source documents, authored by chroniclers both famous and little known. The texts in the History Firsthand series comprise the celebrated and familiar words of the presidents, generals, and famous men and women of letters who recorded their impressions for posterity, as well as the statements of the ordinary people who struggled to understand the storm of events around them—the foot soldiers who fought the great battles and their loved ones back home, the men and women who waited on the breadlines, the college students who marched in protest.

The texts in this series are particularly suited to students beginning serious historical study. By examining these firsthand documents, novice historians can begin to form their own insights and conclusions about the historical era or event under investigation. To aid the student in that process, the texts in the History Firsthand series include introductions that provide an overview of the era or event, timelines, and bibliographies that point the serious student toward key historical works for further study.

The study of history commences with an examination of words—the testimony of witnesses who lived through an era or event and left for future generations the task of making sense of their accounts. The Greenhaven Press History Firsthand series invites the beginner historian to commence the process of historical investigation by focusing on the words of those individuals who made history by living through it and recording their experiences firsthand.

Introduction: A Period of Rebirth

The Renaissance began in Italy in the mid–fourteenth century as a revolution in artistic, philosophical, and scientific thought, and quickly spread throughout southern Europe. It took another hundred years and the invention of the printing press in the fifteenth century to push it into more conservative northern Europe, where it took on a decidedly more religious interpretation, giving birth to Protestantism and changing forever the structure of world politics. Though the beginning and end of the Renaissance cannot be dated exactly, most scholars agree that the greatest achievements of the age fall between 1350 and 1600.

Although this era began in Italy, the term *renaissance* comes from a French word meaning "rebirth." What was reborn during this time was an appreciation for the ideals presented in the classical literature of the ancient Greeks and Romans. Much of their ancient wisdom and scholarship had been lost or forsaken since the fall of the Roman Empire in the fifth century. But in the eleventh, twelfth, and thirteenth centuries, the Christian Church instigated the Crusades, military campaigns based on religious claims in which massive armies invaded the Holy Land to take it away from the Muslims. These battles brought European soldiers in contact with unfamiliar cultures of the Middle East and North Africa. During their ransacking of libraries in these regions, the Christian armies uncovered many ancient Greek and Roman texts thought to have been destroyed long ago. When these texts were brought back to Europe, scholars began the monumental task of translating the works and rediscovering their own past.

Renaissance scholars mined these classical works for their valuable teachings as well as their artistic merit. Ultimately, these texts and an appreciation for all things classical influenced all spheres of life. Renaissance physicians looked to the ancient Greek physicians Hippocrates (460–377 B.C.) and Galen (c. A.D. 129–200). Astronomers consulted Aristotle's theories on the motion of heavenly bodies. Architects adopted the colonnaded buildings of ancient Greece. Mathematicians studied the works of Euclid (330–260 B.C.). Artists and sculptors rendered characters from Greek mythology. In politics, the Greek concept of democracy was reconsidered. The result of this renewed interest in the classics was an unprecedented flourishing throughout Europe of art, literature, architecture, education, and philosophy, as well as the beginning of modern science.

Origins of the Renaissance

Before such radical changes in society could take hold, the people first had to anxiously desire a change. The new Renaissance philosophy was as much a reaction to the brutal hardships of daily life in the Middle Ages (c. 395–1500) as it was an endorsement of ancient Greek and Roman ideals. Not only did most peasants endure subsistence diets and little hope of improvement, but numerous wars ripped and clawed through Europe during the fourteenth century. The Hundred Years' War, begun in the 1350s, between England and France left many dead, as did various other territorial wars and skirmishes. Perhaps the final straw was the onslaught of the bubonic plague, called the Black Death. Between 1348 and 1350, the plague killed at least one-quarter, and perhaps as much as one-third, of Europe's population. This social devastation had two primary side effects. First, the massive suffering in Europe made many people less willing to accept the church's admonishment that hardships on earth should be silently endured as the price of spiritual progress. Second, the decrease in population caused severe shortages in the workforce.

Throughout the Middle Ages, the dominant economic structure was feudalism, in which monarchs deeded large tracts of land to nobles in exchange for military and financial support. The lords of these lands trained as knights, raised armies, and built castles from which they managed their fields and forests and the masses of peasants who worked those lands. The peasants were indentured servants with little to show for their hard labor. The plague's decimation of the population allowed the surviving peasants to demand more money for their work, money that some used to buy their freedom from the lord as well as a small parcel of their own land, whose yields were theirs to keep or sell. This considerably reduced the nobles' income and weakened their influence with the king.

Faced with these difficulties, monarchs increased their own power through taxation, which allowed them to raise armies without depending on knights. The introduction of gunpowder from Asia at this time made the common soldier more powerful than the highly trained knights, which further decreased the value of the nobility. National armies now became a fact throughout Europe and the nobles who had once wielded such power over the monarchs were reduced to joining the armies themselves because they needed the pay.

The Spirit of Humanism

The breakdown of feudalism helped nurture the Renaissance ideals by creating stronger rulers who were more likely to challenge the Holy Roman Church, which had dictated European values throughout the Middle Ages, and by fostering an attitude among people that they deserved more out of life than the limitations dictated by their birth into a specific social class. Both conditions were necessary to break from the entrenched traditions of the Middle Ages. Intent on making a clear distinction between their "modern" way of looking at the world and the medieval worldview that had prevailed for so many centuries, Renaissance scholars and artists embraced two ancient ideals as the foundation for the Renaissance: the belief that people could control their own destinies, and the belief that the sensual pleasures of life should be celebrated rather than denied. Both concepts were contrary to the teachings of the church and so were a radical departure in this new age. But a radical departure from the dour, restrictive teachings is just what the people were looking for. Dutch priest Desiderius Erasmus (1466?–1536), considered by most historians a founding father of the Renaissance, referred to the coming era with unbridled enthusiasm: "Immortal God, what a world I see dawning! Why can I not grow young again?"[1]

The men and women who envisioned this glorious dawning pursued the study of Latin and Greek in an effort to recover knowledge from the long-overlooked classical texts. In imitation of the ancients, early Renaissance thinkers emphasized the study of subjects that related to human over spiritual concerns. This new focus of learning was dubbed *humanitas* (humanism) by Italian scholar Leonardo Bruni (1370–1444), and those who practiced it were called humanists. The study of "humanities" included language, literature, art, history, rhetoric, and philosophy. For a person to be considered a true humanist, or a "Renaissance man," it was important to become well versed in all these subjects. Historian Augustin Renaudet offers this broad description of humanism:

> The name of humanism can be applied to an ethic based on human nobility. Turned towards both study and action, it recognizes and exalts the greatness of human genius and the power of its creations, opposing its strength to the brute force of inanimate nature. What is essential remains the individual's effort to develop in himself or herself, through strict and methodical discipline, all human faculties, so as to lose nothing of what enlarges and enhances the human being. . . . It lays the foundations of individual and collective morality; it establishes law and creates an economy; it produces a political system; it nourishes art and literature.[2]

Such a diverse education, it was argued, would allow a person to break from the stranglehold of traditional values and envision the world in light of new possibilities. Often these new beliefs directly defied the church. Medieval religious teachings stressed that the meaning of life was to be found in concentrating on the afterlife and therefore rejected individual achievement in the arts. According to church doctrine, humans were born sinners and therefore had little power to affect their destiny. The humanists of the Renaissance, however, chose to emphasize the potential of the individual. Looking back to the ancient Greek and Roman civilizations, golden ages of individual human achievement, humanists celebrated the human spirit, stressing free will and declaring that each person had the power to shape his or her own destiny. Whereas in the Middle Ages the human body, with all its unruly desires and frailties, was viewed as an obstacle to spiritual growth, the humanists saw the body as a glorious reflection of the pure spirit within, an expression of God's grace.

The Search for New Worlds

The spread of the humanist ideals of the Renaissance was financed by an economic boom spurred by the growth of trade. Between 1400 and 1600, many powerful European countries competed to discover new trade routes to foreign lands. They hoped to find new products to sell at home as well as develop new markets abroad to sell the goods they brought from their own countries. This fierce competition resulted in an unprecedented era of European colonialism.

National treasuries bulged with riches. The Spanish conquistadors who pillaged North and South America paid a portion of their profits to the Spanish Crown. All conquered land was owned by Spain and all goods coming in were heavily taxed. Other European countries followed the same basic pattern and also became significantly wealthier. That wealth allowed them to build large, well-equipped armies that gave them more independence from the influence of the church. This did not mean they severed all ties with the papacy in Rome; rather, the popes could no longer dictate policy without consulting, and in some case acquiescing to the wishes of these powerful monarchs.

Spain and Portugal, powerful Catholic kingdoms, were the early leaders in foreign exploration. Portugal's Prince Henry the Navigator (1394–1460) was so dedicated to this pursuit that he established a maritime academy to teach sailors all that was known about navigation, instruments, and sailing. Portugal stumbled on and conquered the land known today as Brazil. The Portuguese also founded trading posts in India, West Africa, and Southeast Asia. Spain followed Portugal's lead and in 1492 financed Christopher Columbus's search for a shortcut to India. Columbus accidentally landed in America and claimed it for Spain. Eventually, Spain took control of most of Latin America and parts of North America and thrived on the gold and silver mined in Mexico and Peru. The competition between Portugal and Spain to claim new territories became so fierce that in 1493, in order to avoid wars, Pope Alexander VI (1431–1503) used his spiritual authority to divide the entire world between Portugal and Spain. Spain received the Western Hemisphere and Portugal the Eastern Hemisphere. However, the two countries soon argued over boundaries and the agreement fell apart.

As the rise of Protestantism further weakened the authority of the church, other European nations joined the rush to explore. Along with Spain and Portugal, the most aggressive colonialist countries were England, France, and the Netherlands. The English laid claim to vast areas of India and Africa, as well as parts of North America, establishing the original thirteen colonies that would become the United States. At the same time, France and the Netherlands were also staking out territory in North America.

The spread of colonialism brought great financial rewards but entailed many costs. Constant battles with native peoples resulted in devastating losses of life. The lofty democratic principles of the Renaissance were not applied to the natives of lands that the monarchs wished to colonize. Treated as backward inferiors, these natives were often brutalized, enslaved, or slaughtered.

Many natives who were not enslaved and did not die defending their lands against the intruders often succumbed to European diseases against which they had no defense. At first, introduction of new diseases was accidental, but later, in an early example of germ warfare, settlers knowingly traded goods such as blankets infected with smallpox, wiping out entire native tribes. In 1500 the population in the Spanish territories in the New World was about 50 million. By 1650, even with the influx of Spanish immigrants, the population had fallen to only 4 million.

The great European powers also battled one another for possession of Asian and New World territories. The English, French, Portuguese, and Dutch, for example, fought over control of India throughout the Renaissance. War was considered just another cost of doing business, and business was good.

The Rise of the Merchant Class

The new prosperity extended beyond royal treasuries. Bankers and traders also became wealthy, creating a merchant class with increasing influence over the monarchy. Medieval notions of social class and mobility changed as those born into common families became richer and more powerful. This newly literate and influential class were eager to reject medieval ways of thinking that had hampered their progress and embrace the new ideals of humanism that declared each person should achieve according to his ability and talent, not social class. In medieval times, a person's profession, and therefore monetary success, generally depended on his social status, which was dictated by his birth and family status. However, during the Renaissance, this rigid division of social class began to break down, though not altogether disintegrate. A person was much more likely to be able to enter a profession and become successful based on talent alone. According to historians Wallace Ferguson and Geoffrey Bruun:

> In the rapidly shifting politics of the Italian cities, nobility of birth was not essential to power; the new capitalistic methods of business enabled some men to accumulate wealth far beyond their fellows; and the generous patronage of art raised lowborn artists high above the level of the ordinary artisan. There seemed no limit to what man might accomplish, aided only by fortune and his own ability.[3]

The opportunity for these men to become successful de-

pended also on the rise of prosperous city-states in northern
Italy. At that time, there was no nation of Italy as it exists today. Rather, various city-states, including Milan, Rome, Florence, and Venice, existed as independent political entities.
This urban society, as opposed to the agriculture-based so-
cieties prominent elsewhere in Europe, became the basis for
Renaissance economic growth. Italy's economic prosperity
began with its fortunate geographic position in the Mediterranean Sea, which allowed Italian city-states to monopolize
the trade between eastern Mediterranean lands and western
Europe. Eastern goods such as spices, silk, cotton, sugar, and
dye could not be produced in Europe, so each imported boat-
load was worth a fortune. Many Italian merchants amassed
large amounts of capital, which they then invested in other
businesses. Investing provided a more stable economic com-

Renaissance Italy

munity, less reliant on high-risk trading in which ships could be sunk by passing storms and entire fortunes ruined. As Ferguson and Bruun note, the flourishing city-states became centers of culture and high society, attracting nobles to abandon their remote castles and move into the cities:

> Leaving their isolated rural castles, they moved into the cities and became the neighbors of non-noble burghers. In this urban society, in which all classes were represented, medieval and class distinctions inevitably became less pronounced. Birth still meant a great deal, but wealth or political power might mean more; and where they were lacking, literary, artistic, or any other outstanding ability was sufficient to gain entry into the homes of the noble or rich.[4]

As the city-states became wildly successful in trading and banking, a new class of rich businessmen evolved. This merchant class demanded literacy, not just of themselves, but also of many of their employees. This produced a large number of educated laypersons who enjoyed literature and art, thus creating a demand that new humanist artists were ready to fill.

New Artistic Attitudes

Flush with capital from the trading boom, wealthy businessmen hired architects to erect magnificent new buildings and artists to adorn them with bold new artworks. The most powerful of these patrons was the Medici family, wealthy bankers who ruled Florence for several generations. Because they sponsored so many new artists, Florence became the center of Renaissance art and architecture. Before this time, most of the art and architecture was commissioned by the church or state (with the state heavily influenced by the church). Therefore, the subject matter was usually religious, and could be presented only in a manner approved by the church. However, with so many newly wealthy individuals patronizing art, the subject matter became more secular and artists were now free to explore different artistic techniques.

The first to make a break with medieval artistic traditions was Florence's Giotto (1276–1336), whose use of realism stunned the public and spawned several generations of imitators. But his followers still depicted mostly religious subjects. Not until the fifteenth century did more secular subject matter become popular, led by three Florentine painters: Masaccio (1402–1429?), the first to introduce humanism into painting; Fra Filippo Lippi (1406–1469), who painted Florentine citizens in scenes of the Holy Family; and Sandro Botticelli (1447–1510), whose *Birth of Venus* is considered a major example of Renaissance art. These are the major artists whose experiments with secular subjects and technique in realism established the basic rules of Renaissance art.

Following this experimental period came the golden age of Italian Renaissance art, from the end of the fifteenth century through the middle of the sixteenth century. The first master of this age was Florentine Leonardo da Vinci (1452–1519), whose *Mona Lisa* and *Last Supper* emphasized the psychology of character over mere realism. Raphael (1483–1520) is considered less profound but an unsurpassed master at coloring and harmony. His *School of Athens* and *Madonna* were commissioned by the Church for the Sistine Chapel in Rome. Michelangelo (1475–1564), whose sculpture *David* represented Florence's pride and independence at a time when it was threatened by enemy city-states, was persuaded to turn to painting to create the magnificent art of the ceiling of the Sistine Chapel.

Leonardo da Vinci's Mona Lisa

While Italian artists preferred large murals or panel paintings, Renaissance painters of northern Europe emerged with their own style and techniques. In northern France, artists continued the medieval practice of focusing their art on illuminating texts and illustrating books. At the beginning of the fifteenth century, the center of art in northern Europe was the Netherlands. Jan van Eyck (c. 1390–1441) was an innovator in the versatile use of oil paints. He filled canvases with near-photographic detail of mirror reflections of people, objects, and clothing. His successors, Roger van der Weyden (1400–1464) and Hans Memling (c. 1430–1494), used the same realism, but added more human drama to their subjects. German Albrecht Dürer (1471–1528) adopted Italian Renaissance techniques to his own style, producing numerous paintings, drawings, woodcuts, and engravings that displayed a concern with religious and moral issues.

Writers of the Renaissance

The rise of an educated merchant class created a market for literature as well as art. Florentine poet Petrarch (1304–1374) is credited with being the first great writer of the Renaissance. His introspective verse, which broke from the past in making poetry more personal, more about humanist notions of individual feelings and less about impersonal moral lessons, had a great influence of the writers to follow. While Petrarch shaped the style of poetry, fellow Italian Giovanni Boccaccio (1313–1375) shaped the style of prose in his funny and bawdy stories in the *Decameron*. Less introspective than Petrarch, Boccaccio nevertheless presented a dynamic and detailed description of the people of the time, which made his work a model for subsequent novelists.

Nonfiction writers of influence include Niccolò Machiavelli (1469–1527), a Florentine historian whose political treatise *The Prince* (c. 1513) is considered one of the first works of political science. In it, he offers advice to any ruler who wishes to be successful, suggesting that honesty, compassion, and morality be abandoned in favor of the practical rule in which the end justifies the means. Although the book offers teachings that disregard typical humanist beliefs, Machiavelli uses both classical sources and critical reasoning to formulate his teachings, a technique reflecting the virtues of Renaissance thinking. Another Italian, Baldassare Castiglione (1478–1529), also wrote a book of instruction

(*The Courtier*), but Castiglione intended to teach those who attended the royal court how to behave properly. His book became a best-seller throughout Europe, influencing courtiers in every country.

The most renowned Renaissance writer, English playwright William Shakespeare (1564–1616), filled his works with the humanist ideals of previous Renaissance writers. He explored human emotions, examined notions of free will, and glorified the potential of humans to endure hardships and achieve greatness through their own desire. At that same time, the world's first novel, *Don Quixote*, was being written by Spain's Miguel de Cervantes (1547–1616). In it he satirizes medieval codes of conduct while promoting humanist beliefs.

The Printing Press

While artists and writers expressed the ideals of the Renaissance, the rise of the educated merchant class in Italy provided concrete evidence that many could benefit from those ideals. And as the economic boom spread throughout southern Europe, Renaissance ideals found new and receptive audiences in other countries. However, northern Europe was more entrenched in the traditions of the Middle Ages and change came slowly. It took a hundred years for Renaissance ideals to cross the Alps and inspire a new generation of humanists in northern Europe, and the brand of humanism they came to practice was not the same as that of the Italians. Northern Europeans were more religious-minded than the secular Italians. So, when they embraced humanism, it was in order to lead a more moral life. They did reject the restrictions and corruption of the church, but they did not abandon their Christian ideals. And though they studied the ancient Greek and Roman texts, they continued to steep themselves in the Bible.

The printing press invented by German goldsmith Johannes Gutenberg (c. 1400–1468) around 1451 allowed for mass distribution throughout Europe of humanist ideas, beliefs, and philosophies. Before the invention of movable type and mechanized printing presses, books were handwritten and therefore expensive, inaccurate, and not readily available. Gutenberg created a machine that printed many copies of inked pages assembled by rearranging durable metal letters. Books and pamphlets could be churned out by the hundreds in a short time far more cheaply. Ferguson and Bruun describe the monumental impact of the printing press:

> The effects of the printing press on the general intellectual development of Europe can scarcely be overestimated. Its immediate result for the spread of humanism in the north was to place the writings of Christian antiquity at the disposal of all who could read them, at a moderate price, and to afford the humanists themselves a far wider audience than would have been possible before.[5]

Within a few years of the development of the printing press, the number of books available increased dramatically and the cost of a book dropped to an eighth of what it had been before. By the end of the fifteenth century more than a thousand printers were employed in the trade and more than thirty thousand different titles had been published. In

Johannes Gutenberg's invention of the printing press increased the availability of books dramatically during the Renaissance.

northern Europe, where there were fewer wealthy people to afford handwritten books, and libraries were greater distances apart, the Renaissance might have stalled for decades, if not for good without this development. Historian Charles Van Doren comments on the fortunate circumstances necessary for the movement to blossom:

> It was a remarkable conjunction of events—the new availability of rag paper, the invention of printing with metal movable type, and the sudden appearance of a large number of excellent manuscripts crying out for publication—that propagated the Renaissance. Without these elements, the dream of Petrarch and Boccaccio would have turned out to be very different indeed.[6]

The Reformation of the Catholic Church

The spread of Renaissance humanism into northern Europe gave voice to dissatisfaction that some laymen and religious scholars felt with the church. The church had dominated European life, for nearly fifteen centuries, its authority virtually unquestioned. Most monarchs were aligned with the Holy Roman Church, as were their subjects, and no ruler who wished to stay in power could afford to have the church as an enemy. Such great power led to great wealth, and the lure of both led to corruption within the church. As the popes focused less on spiritual matters and more on maintaining their political power and wealth, a group of reformers arose within the church and began an assault that would eventually split the church in two.

The secular humanists and the religious reformers were similar in that both were committed to a philosophy of focusing on life in this world, specifically how to enjoy it and still remain a moral person. Both drew inspiration from earlier historical periods in order to free the people from restrictive beliefs. However, while the humanists studied Greek and Latin texts, the reformers studied Hebrew texts. While the humanists such as Erasmus satirized the abuses of the church, the reformers directly denounced them. Historian John F.H. New describes the differences further:

The [secular] group tolerated the papacy and concentrated its scorn on superstitions and on the medieval religious orders; the [reformers were] alienated by the practice and pretension of the Renaissance papacy. It was not simply that Renaissance popes had been derelict in their duty to cure souls, or that they were politically minded and materialistic, and often guilty of gross nepotism and flagrant immorality. What mattered was the abuse of the spiritual office of the Pope.[7]

The pope's image as God's agent and as a spiritual model for all Christians had been tarnished and reformers were anxious to restore virtue to the papacy.

The dissatisfaction with the church found its voice in Martin Luther (1483–1546), a German monk and scholar at the University of Wittenberg. Following a trip to Rome in 1513, where he witnessed corruption firsthand, Luther compiled a list of grievances, known as the Ninety-Five Theses, which he is famously said to have nailed to the door of All Saints' Church in Wittenberg. The focus of his concern was the church's practice of selling indulgences as a means of raising large sums of money. An indulgence required the penitent to pay a sum of money to the clergy in order to reduce the time his soul would have to spend in

Martin Luther

purgatory. A common rhyme of the time declared that "As soon as the coin the coffer rings / The soul from purgatory springs."[8] Luther argued that salvation came through faith alone and did not require the intervention of a priest. As a result of this challenge to its authority, the church excommunicated Luther in 1520. But it was already too late; Protestantism, the new religion that embraced Luther's

teachings, was a fact and the power of the church was forever reduced.

No sooner had Protestantism begun then serious theolog-
ical and political conflicts emerged among its practitioners.
Luther himself was at the core of some of the conflicts. He
founded the Lutheran Church, which, though it retained
much old doctrine and practice, was different in several key
ways from the Catholic Church (as the Holy Roman Church
was now called). First, Luther rejected the idea that one had
free will and could do good deeds that would aid in one's
own salvation. Salvation was conveyed through faith alone,
and the Bible the only true authority. Second, he abolished
all sacraments except baptism and the Lord's Supper, the
two rites that are specifically referred to in the Bible. Third,
Lutheran clergy were allowed to marry, as Luther himself
did. Fourth, the monastic orders were disbanded. Many
Christian humanists, led by Erasmus, who had previously
supported Luther, became disillusioned with this new
church, especially because of its denial of free will and a
person's ability to achieve his own salvation, major principles of Renaissance humanism. Without the support of these
humanists, the Lutheran Church became even more conservative and dogmatic.

Luther also quickly lost the support of German peasants
and poor city workers when he turned against them. Many
peasants had embraced this new religious climate to launch
their own social crusade against their exploitation by the
merchants who made more profit selling the farmers' goods
than the farmer did growing them. Meanwhile, the knights
and nobles who were caught in financial straits of their own
began demanding more money from the peasants who
worked their lands, leading to the Peasants' War of 1525.
Such revolts had broken out periodically for two hundred
years; the difference in 1525 is explained by historians Ferguson and Bruun:

> What made the peasant rebellion at once more general and more
> radical was that the peasants had found, in Luther's assertion that

the Bible is the only real authority, a justification for revolt and a program of social reform that would unite the discontented elements of different parts of the country in a common movement. Their dream of restoring the social conditions of evangelical Christianity was impractical, but it gave the necessary religious coloring to their demands.[9]

But Luther rejected their demands and sided with the authorities, calling on them to crush the "thievish, murderous hordes of peasants."[10] Over one hundred thousand German peasants were killed in battle or executed later. The nobles, with Luther's support, had won, but Luther had lost vital support.

As Protestantism spread, Catholic rulers fearing its rising political influence often turned to persecuting Protestants. Mary Tudor (1516–1558), who became queen of England in 1553 after the death of her father, Henry VIII (1491–1547), reversed his break from the church to once again make Catholicism the official religion of England. During her decade-long reign, Protestants were routinely burned at the stake. In France, on St. Bartholomew's Eve in 1572, a three-day massacre of Protestants by mobs of Parisians left two thousand dead. Similar massacres in other cities soon took place throughout France. However, this violent backlash was less a religious dispute than a political one. Catholic rulers feared threats to their power, power that depended significantly on the support of the Catholic Church. The rise of Protestantism was the rise of a challenge to all authority, a demand for people to be not only their own priests and to have more control over their spiritual lives, but to have more say over their political lives.

The Catholic Church decided to fight back in what is known as the Counter-Reformation. The Holy Office of Inquisition, a tribunal against which there was no appeal, sent inquisitors to every Catholic country in search of heretics. They had the power to confiscate property and torture suspects regardless of social rank. An Index (officially abandoned only in 1966) was also established, listing works by writers, artists, and printers that were to be banned or burned.

Meanwhile, the church was undergoing a transformation from within. The politically minded popes Julius III and Paul IV were succeeded by the more spiritual Pius V and Sixtus V. Rededication to issues of faith reaffirmed many followers' loyalty. As historians Louis Mazoyer and François Souchal note:

> Thanks to the Counter-Reformation, the Catholic Church succeeded in stemming the advance of Protestantism. . . . The Church emerged from its trials stronger; it was more assured in its doctrine, more conscious of its duties, more firmly under the control of a single head whose prestige had been enhanced. Though two-thirds of Europe had broken loose from its authority, the Catholic Church yet remained a great force.[11]

The End of the Renaissance

No single event started the Renaissance and no single event ended it. Rather, enthusiasm for the teachings of the Renaissance tapered off as people became more complacent about the changes that had been brought about. The world had forever been changed by the humanism of the Renaissance, and though the fire had died down, its principles would continue to flare up on occasion, such as with the spread of democracy. The history of Europe and America for the next four hundred years would be guided by the light of the humanist belief that people had the ability to shape their own destinies, the right to choose those destinies, and the obligation to choose morally.

Notes

1. Quoted in James Bruce Ross and Mary Martin McLaughlin, *The Portable Renaissance Reader*. New York: Viking Press, 1966, p. 1.
2. Quoted in Fernand Braudel, *A History of Civilizations*. New York: Penguin, 1994, p. 340.
3. Wallace Ferguson and Geoffrey Bruun, *A Survey of European Civilization*. 3rd ed. New York: Houghton Mifflin, 1962, p. 324.
4. Ferguson and Bruun, *A Survey of European Civilization*, p. 324.
5. Ferguson and Bruun, *A Survey of European Civilization*, p. 346.

6. Charles Van Doren, *A History of Knowledge.* New York: Ballantine, 1991, p. 155.

7. John F.H. New, *The Renaissance and Reformation: A Short History.* New York: John Wiley & Sons, 1969, p. 116.

8. Quoted in New, *The Renaissance and Reformation,* p. 123.

9. Ferguson and Bruun, *A Survey of European Civilization,* p. 381.

10. Quoted in Ferguson and Bruun, *A Survey of European Civilization,* p. 381.

11. Quoted in Marcel Dunan, ed., *Larousse Encyclopedia of Modern History: From 1500 to the Present Day.* New York: Harper & Row, 1964, p. 58.

Chapter 1

A New Age of Humanism

Chapter Preface

The spirit of the Renaissance was a direct rebellion against the teachings of the Middle Ages. While the Middle Ages had emphasized the study of God, the Renaissance emphasized the study of people. While the Middle Ages stressed living a disciplined life, forgoing earthly pleasures in order to secure a place in heaven, the Renaissance stressed exploring the pleasures of this life in order to secure a better life on earth. These earthly pleasures included not only mere sensual appreciation of eating, drinking, and sexual activity but also the pursuit of a broad education, the appreciation of art, and living a moral life. Those who embraced this philosophy, which they adapted from the ancient Greek and Roman writers, were called "humanists."

This new humanist attitude of celebration was in part a reaction to the many catastrophes, from war to disease, that marked the Middle Ages and therefore shook people's confidence in conventional beliefs and authorities. The devastation of the bubonic plague epidemic, called the Black Death, which killed one-quarter of Europe's population in the mid–fourteenth century, was a prime factor in people's turning to new influences in a search for meaning and positive values. The massive loss of life in these disasters so reduced the workforce that surviving workers were able to demand higher wages and greater independence. This contributed to the collapse of the feudal system, in which peasants were obligated to work land and pay taxes to the knight, baron, or king who owned the land.

Having more personal freedom encouraged people to question other institutions, including the Roman Catholic Church, whose authority throughout Europe was nearly absolute. Corruption within the church became so rampant that people were less inclined to follow its medieval admonishment to rejoice in their poverty while they watched representatives of the church live in luxury. This led to a schism within the church and the founding of Protestantism.

Humanists were anxious to put the horrors and injustices of the past behind them. They wanted their art and literature to reflect a belief in a new age in which people were free to choose their own destinies, regardless of their class. They wanted their scientists to pursue truth, no matter where it led or whom it contradicted. And they wanted their philosophers and religious leaders to spread this hopeful attitude throughout the world.

On the Dignity of Man

Giovanni Pico della Mirandola

Although Giovanni Pico della Mirandola (1463–1494) died
at the early age of thirty-one, his intelligence, courage, and
unbridled curiosity about all things made him both the
embodiment of Renaissance principles and an influence on
other Renaissance figures. As a student, he mastered religion
and philosophy as well as Hebrew, Latin, Greek, Arabic, and
Aramaic. From these diverse sources he created his own
world philosophy, which he expressed in nine hundred propositions about philosophy and religion. At the age of only
twenty-four, he confidently invited the leading scholars of
Europe to come to Rome, where he would defend his propositions against any of their challenges. The "Oration on the
Dignity of Man" excerpted below was composed as an intro-
ductory speech for this occasion.

Pico's major contribution, as displayed in this essay, is his
articulate and passionate expression of the Renaissance's
humanist celebration of free will. This was a clear rejection of
Middle Age teachings that there existed a universal order
("chain of being") that prevented humans from progressing
spiritually without God's intervention. Rather than being
crude creatures with sinful natures, Pico argued that humans
were slightly lower than angels and, though capable of acting
like animals, were also capable of acting like gods.

Excerpted from *Oration on the Dignity of Man*, by Giovanni Pico della Mirandola, translated by A. Robert Caponigri (Chicago: Henry Regnery Company, 1956). Copyright © 1956
by Henry Regnery Company. Reprinted with permission.

M ost esteemed Fathers, I have read in the ancient writings of the Arabians that [eighth-century Arab scholar] Abdala the Saracen on being asked what, on this stage, so to say, of the world, seemed to him most evocative of wonder, replied that there was nothing to be seen more marvelous than man. And that celebrated exclamation of Hermes Trismegistus [Greek name for Egyptian god Thoth, reputed author of prophetic writings], "What a great miracle is man, Asclepius" confirms this opinion.

And still, as I reflected upon the basis assigned for these estimations, I was not fully persuaded by the diverse reasons advanced by a variety of persons for the preeminence of human nature; for example: that man is the intermediary between creatures, that he is the familiar of the gods above him as he is lord of the beings beneath him; that, by the acuteness of his senses, the inquiry of his reason and the light of his intelligence, he is the interpreter of nature, set midway between the timeless unchanging and the flux of time; the living union (as the Persians say), the very marriage hymn of the world, and, by [eleventh-century B.C. second king of Israel] David's testimony [in Psalm 8:6] but little lower than the angels. These reasons are all, without question, of great weight; nevertheless, they do not touch the principal reasons, those, that is to say, which justify man's unique right to such unbounded admiration. Why, I asked, should we not admire the angels themselves and the beatific choirs more? At long last, however, I feel that I have come to some understanding of why man is the most fortunate of living things and, consequently, deserving of all admiration; of what may be the condition in the hierarchy of beings assigned to him, which draws upon him the envy, not of the brutes alone, but of the astral beings and of the very intelligences which dwell beyond the confines of the world. A thing surpassing belief and smiting the soul with wonder. Still, how could it be otherwise? For it is on this ground that man is, with complete justice, considered and called a great miracle and a being worthy of all admiration.

Hear then, oh Fathers, precisely what this condition of

man is; and in the name of your humanity, grant me your benign audition as I pursue this theme.

God the Father, the Mightest Architect, had already raised, according to the precepts of His hidden wisdom, this world we see, the cosmic dwelling of divinity, a temple most august. He had already adorned the supercelestial region with Intelligences, infused the heavenly globes with the life of immortal souls and set the fermenting dung-heap of the inferior world teeming with every form of animal life. But when this work was done, the Divine Artificer still longed for some creature which might comprehend the meaning of so vast an achievement, which might be moved with love at its beauty and smitten with awe at its grandeur. When, consequently, all else had been completed (as both [fourteenth-to thirteenth-century B.C. Hebrew prophet] Moses [in Genesis 2:1] and [third-century B.C. Greek historian] Timaeus testify)[in Plato's *Timaeus*], in the very last place, He bethought Himself of bringing forth man. Truth was, however, that there remained no archetype according to which He might fashion a new offspring, nor in His treasure-houses the wherewithal to endow a new son with a fitting inheritance, nor any place, among the seats of the universe, where this new creature might dispose himself to contemplate the world. All space was already filled; all things had been distributed in the highest, the middle and the lowest orders. Still, it was not in the nature of the power of the Father to fail in this last creative élan; nor was it in the nature of that supreme Wisdom to hesitate through lack of counsel in so crucial a matter; nor, finally, in the nature of His beneficent love to compel the creature destined to praise the divine generosity in all other things to find it wanting in himself.

At last, the Supreme Maker decreed that this creature, to whom He could give nothing wholly his own, should have a share in the particular endowment of every other creature. Taking man, therefore, this creature of indeterminate image, He set him in the middle of the world and thus spoke to him:

"We have given you, Oh Adam, no visage proper to yourself, nor any endowment properly your own, in order that whatever place, whatever form, whatever gifts you may, with premeditation, select, these same you may have and possess through your own judgment and decision. The nature of all other creatures is defined and restricted within laws which We have laid down; you, by contrast, impeded by no such restrictions, may, by your own free will, to whose custody We have assigned you, trace for yourself the lineaments of your own nature. I have placed you at the very center of the world, so that from that vantage point you may with greater ease glance round about you on all that the world contains. We have made you a creature neither of heaven nor of earth, neither mortal nor immortal, in order that you may, as the free and proud shaper of your own being, fashion yourself in the form you may prefer. It will be in your power to descend to the lower, brutish forms of life; you will be able, through your own decision, to rise again to the superior orders whose life is divine."

Oh unsurpassed generosity of God the Father, Oh wondrous and unsurpassable felicity of man, to whom it is granted to have what he chooses, to be what he wills to be! The brutes, from the moment of their birth, bring with them, as [second-century B.C. Roman poet Gaius] Lucilius says, "from their mother's womb" all that they will ever possess. The highest spiritual beings were, from the very moment of creation, or soon thereafter, fixed in the mode of being which would be theirs through measureless eternities. But upon man, at the moment of his creation, God bestowed seeds pregnant with all possibilities, the germs of every form of life. Whichever of these a man shall cultivate, the same will mature and bear fruit in him. If vegetative, he will become a plant; if sensual, he will become brutish; if rational, he will reveal himself a heavenly being; if intellectual, he will be an angel and the son of God. And if, dissatisfied with the lot of all creatures, he should recollect himself into the center of his own unity, he will there, become one spirit with God, in the solitary darkness of the Father, Who is set above all things, himself transcend all creatures.

A Complaint of Peace

Desiderius Erasmus

Dutch priest Desiderius Erasmus (1466?–1536) is considered
one of the greatest scholars of the Renaissance. He edited a
Greek edition of the New Testament, which he then translated
into Latin. More notable than the text itself were his preface
and critical notes, which suggested a need for reform within
the Catholic Church. Though not as outspoken as his friend,
Protestant founder Martin Luther (1483–1546), his eloquence
and intellect when he did write about reforms caused some
within the church to accuse him of being the real architect of
the Reformation that split the Catholic Church. Rather than
write directly about issues, he often chose to use satire, as
with his most famous work, *The Praise of Folly*.

In "A Complaint of Peace Spurned and Rejected by the
Whole World," published in 1517, Erasmus makes his plea for
a new era defined by the main principles of the Renaissance:
universal peace, social justice, education, and Christian ideals.

Peace speaks: If it were to their advantage for men to
shun, spurn, and reject me, although I have done nothing to deserve it, I would only lament the wrong done me
and their injustice; but since in rejecting me they deny themselves the source of all human happiness and bring on themselves a sea of disasters of every kind, I must shed tears
rather for the misery they suffer than for any wrong they do
me. I should have liked simply to be angry with them, but I
am driven to feel pity and sorrow for their plight. To repel
in any way one who loves you is cruel, to reject a benefac-

From "A Complaint of Peace Spurned and Rejected by the Whole World," by Desiderius
Erasmus, *The Erasmus Reader*, translated by Erika Rummel (Toronto: University of
Toronto Press, 1990). Reprinted with permission.

tor is ungrateful, to distress your universal provider and guardian is wicked; but for men to deny themselves all the many remarkable benefits I bring with me, and deliberately to prefer instead a foul morass of manifold evils must surely look like the height of madness. Anger is the proper reaction to criminals, but for men thus hounded by the Furies [in Greek mythology, three goddesses who avenge crime, especially against one's family] what can we do but shed tears? They need our tears for no better reason than that they shed none for themselves; they have no greater unhappiness than in being unaware that they are unhappy, for the mere recognition of the gravity of a disease is a step towards recovery of health.

If then I am Peace, praised aloud by gods and men, the fount and source, the sustainer, amplifier, and preserver of all the good things of heaven or earth; if without me there can be no prosperity, no security, nothing sacred or undefiled, nothing pleasurable for men or acceptable to the gods; if on the other hand war is a kind of encircling ocean of all the evils in the world, if through its inherent wickedness prosperity immediately declines, increase dwindles, towers are undermined, sound foundations are destroyed, and sweetness is embittered; in short, if war is so unholy a thing that it is the greatest immediate destroyer of all piety and religion, if nothing is so unfortunate for men and hateful to the gods, in the name of immortal God I must say this: who would believe those beings to be human or possessed of any spark of sanity when they devote so much expenditure and application, such great effort and artifice, amid so many anxieties and dangers, to rid themselves of me—such as I am—while they are willing to pay the heavy price they do for such a burden of evils?

Peace Is Natural

If I were rejected by wild animals in this way, I could bear it more easily and attribute their hostility towards me to nature, which endowed them with a savage disposition; if I were hateful to dumb cattle I would forgive their ignorance because they have been denied the intelligence which alone can discern my qualities. The shameful and monstrous truth is that Nature has produced only one animal gifted with reasoning power and possessed of divine insight, and created only one fitted for good will and concord, and yet you could put me amongst any wild beasts or dumb cattle and I should find a place there sooner than amongst men.

Even between the many celestial bodies, different as they are in motion and power, throughout so many centuries treaties have been established and maintained. The conflicting forces of the elements are evenly balanced so as to preserve unbroken peace, and despite their fundamental opposition they maintain concord by mutual consent and communication. In the bodies of living creatures we see how faithfully the limbs support each other and how ready they are to provide mutual assistance. And what can be so dissimilar as body and soul? Yet the closeness of the tie with which Nature has bound them together is indeed revealed when they are torn apart. Just as life is nothing other than the union of body and soul, so health is the harmony between all the parts of the body.

Animals, though they lack the faculty of reason, live together peacefully and harmoniously according to their different species; elephants, for example, live in herds, pigs and sheep graze together, cranes and rooks fly in flocks. Storks form their own communities and give us lessons in loyalty, dolphins protect each other with mutual services, and the harmony prevailing in colonies of ants and bees is well known. Shall I give further instances, where reason is lacking but not feeling? You can find friendliness in trees and plants. Some are barren unless they have a male nearby; the vine embraces the elm and the peach welcomes the vine. Even where things lack sense perception of the benefit of peace; though they have no power to perceive, yet they come very close to those having perception because they have life. Nothing could be so insensible as a stone, and yet you could say that stones too have a sense of peace and concord; thus the magnet draws iron to itself and holds it when attracted. Moreover, is there not some agreement between the fiercest of animals? Savage lions do not fight each other, nor does a boar threaten a fellow boar with his murderous tusks; there is peace amongst lynxes, no fighting between snakes, and the concord between wolves has won fame in proverbs. Furthermore, what is even more amazing, the evil spirits who first destroyed the harmony between heavenly beings and mortal men and continue to do so today can still observe a truce amongst themselves and maintain their tyranny by agreement, such as it is.

Humans Have the Highest Capacity for Peace

Only men, for whom concord was so fitting and who have the greatest need of it, are not reconciled to each other by Nature, so powerful and effective in other respects, or united by education; they can be neither bound together by the many advantages of agreement nor persuaded to love each other through their awareness and experience of many powerful evils. All men have the same shape and voice, whereas all other kinds of animal differ very widely in bodily shape; to man alone has been given the power of reason, which is common to all and shared with no other living creature. He is the only animal with the gift of speech, the chief promoter of friendly relationships; the seeds of learning and the virtues alike are implanted in him, along with a mild and gentle disposition which is inclined towards good will between him and his fellows, so that he delights in being loved for himself and takes pleasure in being of service to others—so long as he has not been corrupted by base desires, as if by Circe's [in Greek mythology, an enchantress who turned men into animals] potions, and degenerated from man to beast. Hence it is, I believe, that the word 'humane' is generally applied to anything to do with mutual good will. Man has also the capacity for tears, proof of a disposition which is readily persuaded, so that if some difference has arisen and a cloud has overcast the clear sky of friendship, a reconciliation can easily be achieved.

Nature's Design for Peace

Now take a look at all the reasons Nature has provided for concord. She was not satisfied simply with the attractions of mutual good will; she wanted friendship to be not only enjoyable for man but also essential. So she shared out the gifts of mind and body in a way that would ensure that no one should be provided with everything and not need on occasion the assistance of the lowly; she gave men different and unequal capacities, so that their inequality could be evened out by mutual friendships. Different regions provided different products, the very advantage of which taught exchange between them. To all other creatures she assigned their own armour and weapons for self-protection, but man alone she made weak and unarmed and unable to find safety except in treaties and the need of one man for another. Need created cities, need taught the value of alliance between them, so that with combined forces they could repel the attacks of wild beasts or brigands.

Indeed, there is nothing in human affairs which can be self-sufficient. At the very start of life, the human race would have died out at once if it had not been propagated by conjugal harmony; for man would not be born at all, or would die immediately at birth and lose life as he entered it, if the tiny infant were not helped by the kind hand of the midwife and the kind care of his nurse. To meet the same need, Nature has implanted the glowing spark of family affection, so that parents can love the child they have not yet seen; and to this she has added the reciprocal love of children for their parents, so that in their turn they can relieve the helplessness of the old by their support; and we have what all alike find praiseworthy and the Greeks name so aptly 'mutual affection.' Then there are the ties of kinship and affinity, and similarity of disposition, interests, and appearance amongst several people which is certain to foster good will; many too possess a mysterious kind of spiritual perceptiveness and a marvellous propensity towards reciprocal love, something which the Ancients attributed in admiration to a man's godhead.

So Nature provided all these arguments for peace and concord, so many lures and inducements to draw us towards peace, so many means of coercion. But then what Fury appeared with such harmful powers, to scatter, demolish, and destroy them all and to sow an insatiable lust for fighting in the human heart? If custom did not blunt first our sense of amazement and then our awareness of evil, who would believe that there are men endowed with human reason who thus fight, brawl, and rage against each other in perpetual discord, strife, and war? Finally, they confound everything, sacred and profane, with pillaging, bloodshed, disaster, and destruction; no bond is sufficiently sacred to check them in their frenzy for mutual extinction. Were there nothing else, the common name of 'man' should be sufficient to ensure concord amongst men. But granted that Nature, who is such a powerful influence even on wild animals, can do nothing for men, has Christ no influence at all on Christians? And granted that Nature's teaching may well prove inadequate, although it is highly effective even where there is no perception, since the teaching of Christ is so far superior to Nature's, why does it not bring home to those who profess to follow it the importance of what is especially trying to promote, namely peace and mutual good will? Or at least dissuade men from the wickedness, savagery, and madness of waging war?

The Excellence of This Age

Loys Le Roy

French humanist scholar Loys Le Roy (1510?–1577) was a noted historian who pioneered the study of comparative cultures and translated the works of Greek philosophers Plato and Aristotle. In the following excerpted essay from 1575, Le Roy offers a panoramic view of some of the notable achievements during the Renaissance. As he details the many great accomplishments in art, letters, and science, he emphasizes that these wonderful advancements were taking place throughout Europe and were not confined to any single country. Le Roy sees this as evidence that the Renaissance is the dawning of a new age of learning and understanding that will embrace all nations and people. As a humanist, he gives due credit to the imagination of the people who brought about these remarkable changes, but he also refutes the criticism of some religious leaders by arguing that such discoveries honored God rather than debased church doctrine.

Now just as the Tartars [a group of Central Asian peoples], Turks, Mamelukes [the military class that ruled Egypt between 1254 and 1811], and Persians have by their valour drawn to the East the glory of arms, so we here in the West have in the last two hundred years recovered the excellence of good letters and brought back the study of the disciplines after they had long remained as if extinguished. The sustained industry of many learned men has led to such

success that today this our age can be compared to the most
learned times that ever were. For we now see the languages
restored, and not only the deeds and writings of the ancients
brought back to light, but also many fine things newly discovered. In this period grammar, poetry, history, rhetoric, and
dialectic have been illumined by expositions, annotations,
corrections, and innumerable translations. Never has mathematics been so well known, nor astrology, cosmography
[mapping of the general features of the universe], and navigation better understood. Physics and medicine were not in
a state of greater perfection among the ancient Greeks and
Arabs than they are now. Arms and military instruments were
never so destructive and effective, nor was there equal skill
in handling them. Painting, sculpture, modelling, and architecture have been almost wholly restored. And more could
not possibly have been done in eloquence and jurisprudence.
Even politics, including and controlling everything, which
seemed to have been left behind, has recently received much
illumination. Theology, moreover, the most worthy of all,
which seemed to be destroyed by the sophists, has been
greatly illuminated by the knowledge of Hebrew and Greek;
and the early fathers of the Church, who were languishing in
the libraries, have been brought to light. Printing has greatly
aided this work and has made easier its development.

Since in the course of our discussion and the succession
of times we have now arrived at this age, we shall consider
it henceforth, not with respect to the special excellence of
different countries, but as a whole with regard to the mem-
orable deeds and events within this space of time throughout Europe, Asia, Africa, the new lands, in the Orient, the
Occident, the North, the South, and with regard to the blessings which it has pleased God to distribute among persons
notable in the same period throughout the various countries
of the habitable earth. . . .

Enlightened Rulers

The princes who have done most to revive the arts are
[fifteenth-century founder of the Vatican Library] Pope

Nicholas V and [sixteenth-century Italian ruler] Alfonso King of Naples, who welcomed honourably and rewarded liberally those who presented to them Latin translations of Greek books. The King of France, [sixteenth-century monarch] Francis I, paid the salaries of public professors in Paris, and created a sumptuous library at Fontainebleau, full of all the good books. Without the favour and liberality of the kings of Castile and Portugal, the discovery of the new lands and the voyage to the Indies would not have come about. The Medici [Italian family that ruled Tuscany and Florence during most of the period from 1434 to 1737] lords of Florence, Cosimo and Lorenzo, helped very much, receiving the learned men who came to them from all parts, supporting them honourably; and, sending scholars at their own expense to hunt throughout Greece for the good and ancient books which were being lost, they built up magnificent libraries for the common good.

Revolutionary Inventions

Besides the restoration of ancient learning, now almost complete, the invention of many fine new things, serving not only the needs but also the pleasure and adornment of life, has been reserved to this age. Among these, printing deserves to be put first, because of its excellence, utility, and the subtlety of craftsmanship from which has come the cutting of matrices and fonts, the distribution and composing of type, the making of ink and of balls for putting it on the form, the setting of presses and the way of handling them, of dampening the paper, placing, taking out, and drying the leaves, then gathering them into volumes, going over and correcting the proof, which has already been spoken of. Thus more work is accomplished in one day than many diligent scribes could do in a year. On this account, books, formerly rare and dear, have become common and easy to procure. The invention has greatly aided the advancement of all disciplines. For it seems miraculously to have been discovered in order to bring back to life more easily literature which seemed dead. The invention is attributed to the Germans and began in Mainz; it was then employed in Venice and subsequently spread over all Latin Christendom. . . . The Portuguese, however, who have sailed all over the world, trading in the remote East and North, in China and Cathay, have brought back books printed in the language and writing of the country, saying that printing had long been in use in those parts. This fact has led some to believe that the invention was carried through Tartary [area of Central Asia east of the Caspian Sea] and Muscovy [Russia] to Germany and then communicated to other Christians, to whom the providence of God has especially entrusted the consummation of divine and human wisdom. Deprived of this grace, the Mohammedans [followers of Islam] have en-

---

The Virtues of Tobacco

The Renaissance was distinguished by a seemingly endless series of dazzling inventions and remarkable discoveries. Explorers to the New World brought back with them many new wonders, each presented with an eye to marketing it as a product with which to gain riches. In the following excerpt from the year 1585, Thomas Heriot, a member of a failed attempt to colonize Roanoke, Virginia, for the English, extols the virtues of tobacco, including its health benefits.

There is an herbe which is sowed apart by itselfe, and is called by the inhabitants Uppowoc; in the West Indies it hath divers names, according to the severall places and countreys where it groweth and is used; the Spanyards generally call it Tabacco. The leaves thereof being dried and brought into pouder, they use to take the fume or smoake thereof, by sucking it thorow pipes made of clay, into their stomacke and head; from whence it purgeth superfluous fleame and other grosse humours, and openeth all the pores and passages of the body: by which meanes the use thereof not onely preserveth the body from obstructions, but also (if any be, so that they have not bene of too long continuance) in short time breaketh them; whereby their bodies are notably

tirely rejected printing, not using it at all among themselves, nor permitting the importation of books on their own affairs printed elsewhere in Arabic.

Second praise must be given to the invention of the marine compass, the rose, and the steel needle which, when touched or rubbed on the lodestone, always indicates the point corresponding to the direction where the arctic pole is supposed to be. . . . By this skill the whole ocean has been navigated, innumerable islands found, and a great part of *terra firma* [dry land] discovered in the West and South, unknown to the ancients, and therefore called "the new world," which has been not only conquered but also converted to the Christian religion under the power of Spain. . . .

preserved in health, and know not many grievous diseases, wherewithall we in England are often times afflicted.

This Uppowoc is of so precious estimation amongst them, that they thinke their gods are marvellously delighted therewith: whereupon sometime they make hallowed fires, and cast some of the pouder therin for a sacrifice: being in a storme upon the waters, to pacifie their gods, they cast some up into the aire and into the water: so a weare for fish being newly set up, they cast some therein and into the aire: after an escape from danger, they cast some into the aire likewise: but all done with strange gestures, stamping, sometime dancing, clapping of hands, holding up of hands, and staring up into the heavens, uttering therewithall, and chattering strange words and noises.

We ourselves, during the time we were there, used to sucke it after their manner, as also since our return, and have found many rare and woonderfull experiments of the vertues thereof: of which the relation would require a volume by it selfe: the use of it by so many of late, men and women of great calling, as els, and some learned Physicians also, is of sufficient witnesse.

Jon E. Lewis, ed., *The Mammoth Book of Eye-Witness History*. New York: Carroll & Graf, 1998.

I should willingly give third place to "bombard" or cannonry—which has brought an end to all other military instruments of the past, which it surpasses in force of motion, violence, and speed—if it were not for the fact that it seems invented rather for the ruin than the utility of humankind, the enemy of generous virtue, which it attacks without distinction, breaking and destroying everything it encounters. It was first invented in Germany by a worker in alchemy [the process of trying to turn base metals into gold or silver], and from there it has been carried all over the world; and it seems today to be brought almost to perfection, since they have discovered how to shoot in volleys of several pieces simultaneously, which knock down any place no matter how strong it is in site or height or depth of walls and ramparts. . . .

A Warning to the Future

But now it is time to put an end to this discourse by which we have clearly shown the vicissitude in all human affairs, arms, letters, languages, arts, states, laws, and customs, and how they do not cease to rise and fall, growing better or worse alternately.

For if the memory and knowledge of the past serve as instruction to the present and warning to the future, it is to be feared that since they have now arrived at such great excellence, the power, wisdom, disciplines, books, industry, works, and knowledge of the world may in the future decline as they have done in the past and be destroyed; that the order and perfection of today will be succeeded by confusion, refinement by crudity, learning by ignorance, elegance by barbarism. I foresee already in my mind certain peoples, strange in form, colour, and habits, pouring in upon Europe, as did formerly the Goths [Germanic tribe that invaded Roman Empire in third to fifth century], Huns [warlike Asiatic nomadic people that invaded Europe in fourth to fifth century], Lombards [Germanic people that conquered Italy in the sixth century], Vandals [Germanic people that ravaged Gaul, Spain, and Rome between fifth and sixth century], and

Saracens [nomadic people of Syrian and Arabian deserts], who destroyed our towns, cities, castles, palaces, and churches. They will change our customs, laws, languages, and religion; they will burn our libraries, ruining everything noble they find in the countries they occupy in order to destroy their honour and virtue. I foresee wars springing up in all parts, civil and foreign; factions and heresies arising which will profane all that they touch, human and divine; famine and pestilence menacing mortals; the order of nature, the regulation of the celestial movements, and the harmony of the elements breaking down with the advent of floods on the one hand, excessive heat on the other, and violent earthquakes. And I foresee the universe approaching its end through the one or other form of dislocation, carrying with it the confusion of all things and reducing them to their former state of chaos.

Although things proceed in this way, as the physicists tell us, according to the inevitable law of the world, and have their natural causes, nevertheless their coming about depends chiefly on divine providence, which is above all nature and alone knows the times determined in advance for their decline. For this reason men of good will should not be astounded but should rather take courage, each working faithfully in the vocation to which he is called, in order to preserve as many as possible of the fine things restored or recently invented, the loss of which would be irreparable, and to transmit them to those who come after us just as we have received them from our ancestors; likewise good letters insofar as it shall please God for them to endure. We shall pray Him to preserve from indignities those who worthily profess letters in order that they may persevere in this honourable study, improving the arts and clarifying the truth to His praise, honour, and glory.

The Advancement of Learning

Francis Bacon

England's Sir Francis Bacon (1561–1626) was a historian, lawyer, essayist, scientist, philosopher, and statesman. So remarkable were his accomplishments that, for a while, a few historians even thought he might be the secret author of William Shakespeare's plays. His breadth of personal achievement characterized the ideal Renaissance Man, while his advocating of inductive reasoning and scientific observation characterized the Renaissance Age.

While Bacon's most celebrated work is the *New Organon*, which presents his scientific method for inquiry and experimentation, *The Advancement of Learning*, dedicated to England's King James I and excerpted below, is an impassioned plea for a new way of observing the world, a way that embodied the Renaissance attitude of seeking truth. Bacon rejects the Middle Ages notion that equated the seeking of scientific knowledge with the sin of pride, which compelled Adam and Eve to eat the forbidden fruit. In the following selection he specifically cautions against intermingling the study of God's word (the Bible) with the study of God's works (the natural world). He calls for a "new birth of science," which meant putting aside traditional cultural and religious notions of how the natural world worked, and being open to whatever new discoveries about nature awaited.

Excerpted from *The Advancement of Learning*, by Francis Bacon (Oxford: Clarendon Press, 1974).

1. To clear the way, and as it were to make silence, to have the true testimonies concerning the dignity of learning to be better heard, without the interruption of tacit objections; I think good to deliver [learning] from the discredits and disgraces which it hath received, all from ignorance; but ignorance severally [variously] disguised; appearing sometimes in the zeal and jealousy of divines; sometimes in the severity and arrogancy of politiques [politicians]; and sometimes in the errors and imperfections of learned men themselves.

2. I hear the former sort say, that knowledge is of those things which are to be accepted of with great limitation and caution: that the aspiring to overmuch knowledge was the original temptation and sin whereupon ensued the fall of man: that knowledge hath in it somewhat of the serpent, and therefore where it entereth into a man it makes him swell; *Scientia inflat* [1 Corinthians 8:1 'Knowledge puffeth up.']: that [tenth-century B.C. King of Israel] Salomon gives a censure, 'That there is no end of making books, and that much reading is weariness of the flesh'; and again in another place, 'That in spacious knowledge there is much contristation, and that he that increaseth knowledge increaseth anxiety': that Saint Paul gives a caveat, 'That we be not spoiled through vain philosophy' [Colossians 2:8]: that experience demonstrates how learned men have been arch-heretics, how learned times have been inclined to atheism, and how the contemplation of second causes doth derogate from our dependence upon God, who is the first cause [God is the first cause, or creator, of the universe].

God Has Framed the Mind of Man

3. To discover then the ignorance and error of this opinion, and the misunderstanding in the grounds [fundamental principles] thereof, it may well appear these men do not observe or consider that it was not the pure knowledge of nature and universality [the whole world], a knowledge by the light whereof man did give names unto other creatures in Paradise, as they were brought before him, according unto their

proprieties [particular natures], which gave the occasion to the fall: but it was the proud knowledge of good and evil, with an intent in man to give law unto himself, and to depend no more upon God's commandments, which was the form of the temptation. Neither is it any quantity of knowledge, how great soever, that can make the mind of man to swell; for nothing can fill, much less extend the soul of man, but God and the contemplation of God; and therefore Salomon, speaking of the two principal senses of inquisition, the eye and the ear, affirmeth that 'the eye is never satisfied with seeing, nor the ear with hearing' [Ecclesiastes 1:8]; and if there be no fulness, then is the continent greater than the content [is that which contains greater than that which is contained]: so of knowledge itself, and the mind of man, whereto the senses are but reporters, he . . . concludeth thus: 'God hath made all things beautiful, or decent, in the true return of their seasons: Also he hath placed the world in man's heart, yet cannot man find out the work which God worketh from the beginning to the end' [Ecclesiastes 3:1–11]: declaring not obscurely, that God hath framed the mind of man as a mirror or glass, capable of [able to receive] the image of the universal world, and joyful to receive the impression thereof, as the eye joyeth to receive light; and not only delighted in beholding the variety of things and vicissitude of times, but raised also to find out and discern the ordinances and decrees, which throughout all those changes are infallibly observed. And although he doth insinuate that the supreme or summary law of nature, which he calleth, 'The work which God worketh from the beginning to the end', is not possible to be found out by man; yet that doth not derogate [detract] from the capacity of the mind, but may be referred to the impediments, as of shortness of life, ill conjunction of labours, ill tradition of knowledge over from hand to hand, and many other inconveniences, whereunto the condition of man is subject. For that nothing parcel [no part] of the world is denied to man's inquiry and invention, he doth in another place rule over [lay down authoritatively], when he saith, 'The spirit of man is as the lamp of God, wherewith he searcheth the inwardness of all secrets' [Proverbs 20:27]. If then such be the capacity and receipt of the mind of man, it is manifest that there is no danger at all in the proportion or quantity of knowledge, how large soever, lest it should make it swell or outcompass itself; no, but it is merely the quality of knowledge, which, be it in quantity more or less, if it be taken without the true corrective thereof, hath in it some nature of venom or malignity, and some effects of that venom, which is ventosity [inflated] or swelling. This corrective spice, the mixture whereof maketh knowledge so sovereign [potent], is charity, which the Apostle [St. Paul] immediately addeth to the former

Sir Francis Bacon

clause: for so he saith, 'Knowledge bloweth up, but charity buildeth up' [I Corinthians 8:1]; not unlike unto that which he delivereth in another place: 'If I spake', saith he, 'with the tongues of men and angels, and had not charity, it were but as a tinkling cymbal' [I Corinthians 13:1]; not but that it is an excellent thing to speak with the tongues of men and angels, but because, if it be severed from charity, and not referred to the good of men and mankind, it hath rather a sounding and unworthy glory, than a meriting [deserving] and substantial virtue.

Three Strictures of Knowledge

And as for that censure of Salomon [Ecclesiastes 12:12], concerning the excess of writing and reading books, and the anxiety of spirit which redoundeth from knowledge; and that admonition of Saint Paul, 'That we be not seduced by vain philosophy' [Colossians 2:8]; let those places be rightly understood, and they do indeed excellently set forth the true bounds and limitations, whereby human knowledge is confined and circumscribed; and yet without any such contracting or coarctation [restriction], but that it may comprehend all the universal nature of things; for these limitations are three: the first, 'That we do not so place our felicity in knowledge, as we forget our mortality': the second, 'That we make application of our knowledge, to give ourselves repose and contentment, and not distaste or repining': the third, 'That we do not presume by the contemplation of nature to attain to the mysteries of God.' For as touching the first of these, Salomon doth excellently expound himself in another place of the same book, where he saith: 'I saw well that knowledge recedeth as far from ignorance as light doth from darkness; and that the wise man's eyes keep watch in his head, whereas the fool roundeth about [roams about] in darkness: but withal I learned, that the same mortality involveth them both.' [Ecclesiastes 2:13–14] And for the second, certain it is, there is no vexation or anxiety of mind which resulteth from knowledge otherwise than merely by accident; for all knowledge and wonder (which is the seed of knowledge) is an impression of pleasure in itself: but when men fall to framing conclusions out of their knowledge, applying it to their particular [own individual case], and ministering to themselves thereby weak fears or vast desires, there groweth that carefulness [anxiety] and trouble of mind. . . . And as for the third point, it deserveth to be a little stood upon, and not to be lightly passed over: for if any man shall think by view and inquiry into these sensible and material things to attain that light, whereby he may reveal unto himself the nature or will of God, then indeed is he spoiled by vain philosophy: for the contemplation of God's creatures and works produceth (having regard to the works and creatures themselves) knowledge, but having regard to God, no perfect knowledge, but wonder, which is broken knowledge [fragmentary or disjointed knowledge]. And therefore it was most aptly said by one of Plato's school [first-century B.C. Jewish philosopher Philo], 'That the sense of man carrieth a resemblance with the sun, which (as we see) openeth and revealeth all the terrestrial globe; but then again it obscureth and concealeth the stars and celestial globe: so doth the sense discover natural things, but it darkeneth and shutteth up divine.' And hence it is true that it hath proceeded [resulted], that divers great learned men have been heretical, whilst they have sought to fly up to the secrets of the Deity by the waxen wings of the senses [refers to the myth of Icarus, whose wings were held together with wax. He flew too close to the sun, which melted the wax, and sent him falling into the sea]. And as for the conceit [conception] that too much knowledge should incline a man to atheism [atheism at this time did not refer to those who did not believe in God's existence, but to those who did not believe God transcended Creation], and that the ignorance of second causes should make a more devout dependence upon God, which is the first cause; first, it is good to ask the question which Job asked of his friends: 'Will you lie for God, as one man will do for another, to gratify him?' [Job 13:7–9] For certain it is that God worketh nothing in nature but by second causes: and if they would have it otherwise believed, it is mere imposture, as it were in favour towards God [for God's sake]; and nothing else but to offer to the author of truth the unclean sacrifice of a lie. But further, it is an assured truth, and a conclusion of experience, that a little or superficial knowledge of philosophy may incline the mind of man to atheism, but a further proceeding therein doth bring the mind back again to religion. . . . To conclude therefore, let no man upon a weak conceit of sobriety [sobermindedness] or an ill-applied moderation think or maintain, that a man can search too far, or be too well studied in the book of God's word, or in the book of God's works, divinity or philosophy; but rather let men endeavour an endless progress or proficience in both; only let men beware that they apply both to charity, and not to swelling [inflation by pride, vanity]; to use, and not to ostentation; and again, that they do not unwisely mingle or confound these learnings together.

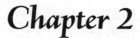

Chapter 2

Politics and Exploration

Chapter Preface

No matter how noble the Renaissance ideals of humanism might have seemed at the time, without the economic boom that began in the fourteenth century to finance its greatest artists and writers and build its cities and trade empires, those ideals might have withered away in obscurity. Instead, strategically located trading ports, like those in Italy, generated huge profits, inspiring several European monarchs to begin exploring the uncharted seas for more trade routes.

Although in the past daring explorers, particularly Norsemen, had ventured far from European bases, none had dispelled the common belief that the waters past Morocco boiled because of liquid fire from the sun, while the waters to the west turned into perilous swamps. To prepare sailors for such hazards, the prince of Portugal, known as Henry the Navigator (1394–1460), founded a maritime center and observatory to teach sailors. Under his patronage, Portugal quickly leaped to the forefront of exploration during the fifteenth century, colonizing parts of Africa and eventually India. England, Spain, France, and the Netherlands also began to vigorously explore other parts of the world, leading to the colonizing of North and South America. Christopher Columbus stumbled upon the Americas in search of a trade route to India, but that error brought enormous riches to Spain and encouraged even more exploration and colonization.

Although the profits from these expeditions helped spread the Renaissance ideals of humanism, equality, and reason among Europeans, when it came to natives of the countries they were colonizing, no such philosophy was followed. The conventional medieval religious teachings that claimed that uncivilized, non-Christian beings were less than human were followed, thereby excusing brutal acts of pillaging, enslavement, and genocide. Bartolome de las Casas, the first priest ordained in the Americas, made it his life's work to defend the natives who were exploited.

Nevertheless, trade with these foreign lands brought fortunes not only to national coffers, but to many traders, merchants, and bankers. This gave rise to a middle class who earned their wealth rather than inherited it. These powerful merchant families were less interested in the traditional values which dictated that one should not rise above the social class one was born into, making them more receptive to Renaissance thinking that each person should be rewarded according to merit. Monarchs could no longer afford to ignore their desires.

The growing power of the middle class, though an increasing challenge to monarchs' authority, had an unexpected benefit for rulers. Because the Protestant Reformation against the Holy Roman Church had begun as a groundswell among commoners and the middle class, monarchs now felt free to make decisions contrary to the wishes of the church, knowing they would now have the support of their citizens. The church was still a powerful force, but the Renaissance era marked the beginning of the end of its direct control over politics in foreign countries.

Columbus Reaches the New World

Christopher Columbus

The appetite for scientific truth that distinguished the Renaissance was equaled by the hunger for exploring and claiming "undiscovered" land. Portugal, Spain, England, Holland, and France raced against each other to find new trading routes, new customers to trade with, and new goods, such as coffee, tobacco, and chocolate, to bring back home. Spain's Christopher Columbus (1451–1506) was one of the most successful explorers. Although America probably had been previously visited by the Vikings, the Carthaginians, the Russians, and the Romans, Columbus was the first to successfully exploit the commercial potential by establishing cities and trade routes. Unfortunately, he did not prove to be as good a politician or administrator as he was a sailor and, after several disastrous decisions as governor, Columbus was stripped of his position and sent back to Spain in chains. He did return to America for one final voyage, but the disappointing results left him broken, sickly, and in near poverty.

The following excerpt is from Columbus's log book upon first arriving at what the natives called Guanahani, but what is now thought to be San Salvador, and then on to Cuba. In it, Columbus informs his sponsor, King Ferdinand, of his encounters and his achievements.

Sir, As I know that you will be pleased at the great victory with which Our Lord has crowned my voyage, I write

Excerpted from *The Four Voyages of Columbus*, by Christopher Columbus, edited and translated by Cecil Jane (New York: Dover Publications, Inc., 1988).

this to you, from which you will learn how in thirty-three days, I passed from the Canary Islands to the Indies with the fleet which the most illustrious king and queen, our sovereigns, gave to me. And there I found very many islands filled with people innumerable, and of them all I have taken possession for their highnesses, by proclamation made and with the royal standard unfurled, and no opposition was offered to me. To the first island which I found, I gave the name *San Salvador* [Watling Island], in remembrance of the Divine Majesty, Who has marvellously bestowed all this; the Indians call it 'Guanahani'. To the second, I gave the name *Isla de Santa María de Concepción* [Rum Cay]; to the third, *Fernandina* [Long Island]; to the fourth, *Isabella* [Crooked Island]; to the fifth, *Isla Juana* [Cuba], and so to each one I gave a new name. . . .

The Wondrous Behavior of the Natives

The people of this island, and of all the other islands which I have found and of which I have information, all go naked, men and women, as their mothers bore them, although some women cover a single place with the leaf of a plant or with a net of cotton which they make for the purpose. They have no iron or steel or weapons, nor are they fitted to use them, not because they are not well built men and of handsome stature, but because they are very marvellously timorous. They have no other arms than weapons made of canes, cut in seeding time, to the ends of which they fix a small sharpened stick. And they do not dare to make use of these, for many times it has happened that I have sent ashore two or three men to some town to have speech, and countless people have come out to them, and as soon as they have seen my men approaching they have fled, even a father not waiting for his son. And this, not because ill has been done to anyone; on the contrary, at every point where I have been and have been able to have speech, I have given to them of all that I had, such as cloth and many other things, without receiving anything for it; but so they are, incurably timid. It is true that, after they have been reassured and have lost their fear, they are so guileless and so generous with all they possess, that no one would believe it who has not seen it. They never refuse anything which they possess, if it be asked of them; on the contrary, they invite anyone to share it, and display as much love as if they would give their hearts, and whether the thing be of value or whether it be of small price, at once with whatever trifle of whatever kind it may be that is given to them, with that they are content. I forbade that they should be given things so worthless as fragments of broken crockery and scraps of broken glass, and ends of straps, although when they were able to get them, they fancied that they possessed the best jewel in the world. So it was found that a sailor for a strap received gold to the weight of two and a half *castellanos* [the weight of gold in the coin], and others much more for other things which were worth much less. As for new *blancas* [a copper coin], for them they would give everything which they had, although it might be two or three *castellanos'* weight of gold or an *arroba* [25 lbs. at 14 oz., rather than current 16 oz., to the pound] or two of spun cotton. . . . They took even the pieces of the broken hoops of the wine barrels and, like savages, gave what they had, so that it seemed to me to be wrong and I forbade it. And I gave a thousand handsome good things, which I had brought, in order that they might conceive affection, and more than that, might become Christians and be inclined to the love and service of their highnesses and of the whole Castilian nation, and strive to aid us and to give us of the things which they have in abundance and which are necessary to us. And they do not know any creed and are not idolaters; only they all believe that power and good are in the heavens, and they are very firmly convinced that I, with these ships and men, came from the heavens, and in this belief they everywhere received me, after they had overcome their fear. And this does not come because they are ignorant; on the contrary, they are of a very acute intelligence and are men who navigate all those seas, so that it is amazing how good an account they give of everything, but it is because they have never seen people clothed or ships of such a kind.

And as soon as I arrived in the Indies, in the first island which I found, I took by force some of them, in order that they might learn and give me information of that which there is in those parts, and so it was that they soon understood us, and we them, either by speech or signs, and they have been very serviceable. I still take them with me, and they are always assured that I come from Heaven, for all the intercourse which they have had with me; and they were the first to announce this wherever I went, and the others went running from house to house and to the neighbouring towns, with loud cries of, 'Come! Come to see the people from Heaven!' So all, men and women alike, when their minds were set at rest concerning us, came, so that not one, great or small, remained behind, and all brought something to eat and drink, which they gave with extraordinary affection. In all the island, they have very many canoes, like rowing *fustas* [a light-oared ship of less than three hundred tons], some larger, some smaller, and some are larger than a *fusta* of eighteen benches. They are not so broad, because they are made of a single log of wood, but a *fusta* would not keep up with them in rowing, since their speed is a thing incredible. And in these they navigate among all those islands, which are innumerable, and carry their goods. One of these canoes I have seen with seventy and eighty men in her, and each one with his oar.

In all these islands, I saw no great diversity in the appearance of the people or in their manners and language. On the contrary, they all understand one another, which is a very curious thing [Columbus later discovered there were many languages], on account of which I hope that their highnesses will determine upon their conversion to our holy faith, towards which they are very inclined.

The Geography of the Islands

I have already said how I have gone one hundred and seven leagues in a straight line from west to east along the seashore of the island Juana, and as a result of that voyage, I can say that this island is larger than England and Scotland together [Columbus's estimates were vastly inaccurate; the area of Cuba is 43,000 square miles, while that of England alone is 50,874 square miles], for, beyond these one hundred and seven leagues, there remain to the westward two provinces to which I have not gone. One of these provinces they call 'Avan' [Havana], and there the people are born with tails; and these provinces cannot have a length of less than fifty or sixty leagues, as I could understand from those Indians whom I have and who know all the islands.

The other, Española, has a circumference greater than all Spain [also inaccurate: the circumference of Española is about 1,500 miles, while the coastline of Spain and Portugal is about 1,900 miles], from Colibre, by the sea-coast, to Fuenterabia in Vizcaya, since I voyaged along one side one hundred and eighty-eight great leagues in a straight line from west to east. It is a land to be desired and, seen, it is never to be left. And in it, although of all I have taken possession for their highnesses and all are more richly endowed than I know how, or am able, to say, and I hold them all for their highnesses, so that they may dispose of them as, and as ab-

After sailing for more than a month, Columbus lands on the island of San Salvador on October 11, 1492.

solutely as, of the kingdoms of Castile, in this Española, in the situation most convenient and in the best position for the mines of gold and for all intercourse as well with the mainland here as with that there, belonging to the Grand Khan, where will be great trade and gain, I have taken possession of a large town, to which I gave the name *Villa de Navidad,* and in it I have made fortifications and a fort, which now will by this time be entirely finished, and I have left in it sufficient men [between 38 and 40 men] for such a purpose with arms and artillery and provisions for more than a year, and a *fusta,* and one, a master of all seacraft, to build others, and great friendship with the king of that land, so much so, that he was proud to call me, and to treat me as, a brother. And even if he were to change his attitude to one of hostility towards these men, he and his do not know what arms are and they go naked, as I have already said, and are the most timorous people that there are in the world, so that the men whom I have left there alone would suffice to destroy all that land, and the island is without danger for their persons, if they know how to govern themselves.

More Habits of the Natives

In all these islands, it seems to me that all men are content with one woman, and to their chief or king they give as many as twenty. It appears to me that the women work more than the men. And I have not been able to learn if they hold private property; what seemed to me to appear was that, in that which one had, all took a share, especially of eatable things.

In these islands I have so far found no human monstrosities, as many expected, but on the contrary the whole population is very well-formed, nor are they negroes as in Guinea, but their hair is flowing, and they are not born where there is intense force in the rays of the sun; it is true that the sun has there great power, although it is distant from the equinoctial line twenty-six degrees. In these islands, where there are high mountains, the cold was severe this winter, but they endure it, being used to it and with the help of meats which they eat with many and extremely hot spices. As I have found no monsters, so I have had no report of any, except in an island 'Quaris' [either Dominica or Maria Galante], the second at the coming into the Indies, which is inhabited by a people who are regarded in all the islands as very fierce and who eat human flesh. They have many canoes with which they range through all the islands of India and pillage and take as much as they can. They are no more malformed than the others, except that they have the custom of wearing their hair long like women, and they use bows and arrows of the same cane stems, with a small piece of wood at the end, owing to lack of iron which they do not possess. They are ferocious among these other people who are cowardly to an excessive degree, but I make no more account of them than of the rest. These are those who have intercourse with the women of 'Matinino', which is the first island met on the way from Spain to the Indies, in which there is not a man. These women engage in no feminine occupation, but use bows and arrows of cane, like those already mentioned, and they arm and protect themselves with plates of copper, of which they have much.

In another island, which they assure me is larger than Española, the people have no hair. In it, there is gold incalculable, and from it and from the other islands, I bring with me Indians as evidence.

The Accomplishments of the Voyage

In conclusion, to speak only of that which has been accomplished on this voyage, which was so hasty, their highnesses can see that I will give them as much gold as they may need, if their highnesses will render me very slight assistance; moreover, spice and cotton, as much as their highnesses shall command; and mastic, as much as they shall order to be shipped and which, up to now, has been found only in Greece, in the island of Chios, and the Seignory sells it for what it pleases; and aloe wood, as much as they shall order to be shipped, and slaves, as many as they shall order to be shipped and who will be from the idolaters. And I believe that I have found rhubarb and cinnamon, and I shall find a thousand other things of value, which the people whom I have left there will have discovered, for I have not delayed at any point, so far as the wind allowed me to sail, except in the town of Navidad, in order to leave it secured and well established, and in truth, I should have done much more, if the ships had served me, as reason demanded.

This is enough . . . and the eternal God, our Lord, Who gives to all those who walk in His way triumph over things which appear to be impossible, and this was notably one; for, although men have talked or have written of these lands, all was conjectural, without suggestion of ocular evidence, but amounted only to this, that those who heard for the most part listened and judged it to be rather a fable than as having any vestige of truth. So that, since Our Redeemer has given this victory to our most illustrious king and queen, and to their renowned kingdoms, in so great a matter, for this all Christendom ought to feel delight and make great feasts and give solemn thanks to the Holy Trinity with many solemn prayers for the great exaltation which they shall have, in the turning of so many peoples to our holy faith, and afterwards for temporal benefits, for not only Spain but all Christians will have hence refreshment and gain.

This, in accordance with that which has been accomplished, thus briefly.

Done in the caravel [a light, mobile ship], off the Canary Islands [actually, he was off Santa Maria, one of the Azores], on the fifteenth of February, in the year one thousand four hundred and ninety-three.

At your orders. El Almirante.

A Prince Is Better Feared than Loved

Niccolò Machiavelli

Niccolò Machiavelli (1469–1527) was born in Florence, Italy, where he rose to minor political power at an early age. His career endured many ups and downs, depending upon who was in power at the time. Accused of conspiring against the ruling Medici family, Machiavelli was tortured and imprisoned, though he never confessed and was eventually released. However, as a result, he was never able to recover a political position and remained in near poverty for the rest of his life.

Although Machiavelli's *The Prince* was specifically written to revitalize Machiavelli's diplomatic career, it has since been hailed as the first modern analysis of power as well as condemned as amoral cynicism. The following selection reveals the essence of Machiavelli's theories of leadership: It is best for a leader to be both loved and feared, but since that is generally not practical, fear allows him to govern more effectively. While other Renaissance writers were describing the ideal Renaissance Man as one of compassion and learning, Machiavelli described idealized dictators as iron-fisted rulers who accepted no dissent. His theories became so widespread that his name has evolved into the word "machiavellian," meaning someone who justifies cruel means to achieve seemingly noble ends. *The Prince* did not promote Machiavelli's own career, though it did influence subsequent dictators such as France's Napoléon Bonaparte (1769–1821), Germany's Adolf Hitler (1889–1945), and Russia's Joseph Stalin (1879–1953) and Vladimir Lenin (1870–1924).

Excerpted from *The Prince*, by Niccolò Machiavelli, translated by E.R.P. Vincent (New York: New American Library, 1953).

Proceeding to the other qualities before named, I say that every prince must desire to be considered merciful and not cruel. He must, however, take care not to misuse this mercifulness. [Sixteenth-century duke of Romagna, Italy] Cesare Borgia was considered cruel, but his cruelty had brought order to the Romagna [a region in north-central Italy], united it, and reduced it to peace and fealty [allegiance]. If this is considered well, it will be seen that he was really much more merciful than the Florentine people, who, to avoid the name of cruelty, allowed Pistoia [capital of Pistoia province in north-central Italy] to be destroyed. A prince, therefore, must not mind incurring the charge of cruelty for the purpose of keeping his subjects united and faithful; for, with a very few examples, he will be more merciful than those who, from excess of tenderness, allow disorders to arise, from whence spring bloodshed and rapine [plundering]; for these as a rule injure the whole community, while the executions carried out by the prince injure only individuals. And of all princes, it is impossible for a new prince to escape the reputation of cruelty, new states being always full of dangers. . . .

Nevertheless, he must be cautious in believing and acting, and must not be afraid of his own shadow, and must proceed in a temperate manner with prudence and humanity, so that too much confidence does not render him incautious, and too much diffidence does not render him intolerant.

Safer to Be Feared than Loved

From this arises the question whether it is better to be loved more than feared, or feared more than loved. The reply is, that one ought to be both feared and loved, but as it is difficult for the two to go together, it is much safer to be feared than loved, if one of the two has to be wanting. For it may be said of men in general that they are ungrateful, voluble, dissemblers, anxious to avoid danger, and covetous of gain; as long as you benefit them, they are entirely yours; they offer you their blood, their goods, their life, and their children, as I have before said, when the necessity is remote; but when it approaches, they revolt. And the prince who has relied solely on their words, without making other preparations, is ruined; for the friendship which is gained by purchase and not through grandeur and nobility of spirit is bought but not secured, and at a pinch is not to be expended in your service. And men have less scruple in offending one who makes himself loved than one who makes himself feared; for love is held by a chain of obligation which, men being selfish, is broken whenever it serves their purpose; but fear is maintained by a dread of punishment which never fails.

Still, a prince should make himself feared in such a way that if he does not gain love, he at any rate avoids hatred; for fear and the absence of hatred may well go together, and will be always attained by one who abstains from interfering with the property of his citizens and subjects or with their women. And when he is obliged to take the life of any one, let him do so when there is a proper justification and manifest reason for it; but above all he must abstain from taking the property of others, for men forget more easily the death of their father than the loss of their patrimony. Then also pretexts for seizing property are never wanting, and one who begins to live by rapine will always find some reason for taking the goods of others, whereas causes for taking life are rarer and more fleeting.

Fear Helps Command Armies

But when the prince is with his army and has a large number of soldiers under his control, then it is extremely necessary that he should not mind being thought cruel; for without this reputation he could not keep an army united or disposed to any duty. Among the noteworthy actions of Hannibal is numbered this, that although he had an enormous army, composed of men of all nations and fighting in foreign countries, there never arose any dissension either among them or against the prince, either in good fortune or in bad. This could not be due to anything but his inhuman cruelty, which together with his infinite other virtues, made him always venerated and terrible in the sight of his soldiers, and without it his other virtues would not have sufficed to produce that effect. Thoughtless writers admire on the one hand his actions, and on the other blame the principal cause of them.

And that it is true that his other virtues would not have sufficed may be seen from the case of [third-century B.C. Roman military commander] Scipio [Africanus] (famous

---

Sir Walter Raleigh's Letter to His Wife Before His Execution

The uncertainty of life at court can be seen in the magnificent career of Sir Walter Raleigh (1554–1618), soldier, seaman, writer, explorer. As a favorite of Queen Elizabeth I, he was given great advantages in amassing wealth. Under Elizabeth's successor, James I, Raleigh attacked a Spanish settlement in Guyana, in which his own son was killed. The attack angered James I who was trying to maintain peace with Spain and he had Raleigh executed. In the following letter to his wife before his execution, Raleigh encourages her to remarry and to maintain faith in God. Following the execution, Raleigh's head was embalmed and presented to his wife, as was customary at the time. She is said to have carried it with her for the next twenty-nine years until she died at age eighty-two.

You shall now receive (my deare wife) my last words in these last lines. My love I send you that you may keep it when I am dead, and my councell that you may remember it when I am no more. I would not by my will present you with sorrowes (dear Besse) let them go to the grave with me and be buried in the dust. And seeing that it is not Gods will that I should see you any more in this life, beare it patiently, and with a heart like thy selfe.

First, I send you all the thankes which my heart can conceive, or my words can rehearse for your many travailes, and care taken for me, which though they have not taken effect as you wished, yet my debt to you is not the lesse: but I pay it I never shall in this world.

not only in regard to his own times, but all times of which memory remains), whose armies rebelled against him in Spain, which arose from nothing but his excessive kindness, which allowed more licence to the soldiers than was consonant with military discipline. He was reproached with this in the senate by [third-century B.C. Roman military commander] Fabius Maximus, who called him a corrupter of the

Secondly, I beseech you for the love you beare me living, do not hide your selfe many dayes, but by your travailes seeke to helpe your miserable fortunes and the right of your poor childe. Thy mourning cannot availe me, I am but dust.

Thirdly, you shall understand, that my land was conveyed bona fide to my childe; the writings were drawne at midsumer was twelve months, my honest cosen Brett can testify so much, and Dolberry too, can remember somewhat therein. And I trust my blood will quench their malice that have cruelly murthered me: and that they will not seek also to kill thee and thine with extreme poverty. . . .

Teach your son also to love and feare God while he is yet young, that the feare of God may grow with him, and then God will be a husband to you, and a father to him; a husband and a father which cannot be taken from you. . . .

When I am gone, no doubt you shall be sought for my many, for the world thinkes that I was very rich. But take heed of the pretences of men, and their affections, for they last not but in honest and worthy men, and no greater misery can befall you in this life, than to become a prey, and afterwards to be despised. I spoke not this (God knowes) to dissuade you from marriage, for it will be best for you, both in respect of the world and of God. As for me, I am no more yours, nor you mine, death hath cut us asunder: and God hath divided me from the world, and your from me. . . .

Written with the dying hand of sometimes they Husband, but now alasse overthrowne. Yours that was, but now not my own.

Walter Raleigh

Rich Geib's Humble Outpost in Cyberspace, www. rjgeib.com/thoughts/dust/dust.html.

Roman militia. Locri [city on eastern "toe" of Italy] having been destroyed by one of Scipio's officers was not revenged by him, nor was the insolence of that officer punished, simply by reason of his easy nature; so much so, that some one wishing to excuse him in the senate, said that there were many men who knew rather how not to err, than how to correct the errors of others. This disposition would in time have tarnished the fame and glory of Scipio had he persevered in it under the empire, but living under the rule of the senate this harmful quality was not only concealed but became a glory to him.

I conclude, therefore, with regard to being feared and loved, that men love at their own free will, but fear at the will of the prince, and that a wise prince must rely on what is in his power and not on what is in the power of others, and he must only contrive to avoid incurring hatred, as has been explained.

In Defense of the Indians

Bartolomé de las Casas

Spaniard Bartolomé de las Casas (1474–1566) first came
to the West Indies as a lay evangelist, dedicated to converting
the local natives to Catholicism. In 1512 or 1513, he became
the first person in America to be ordained as a priest. As a
reward for his participation in several expeditions, las Casas
was given land and local natives to serve as slaves. However,
in 1514, moved by the brutal treatment of the natives by the
Spanish conquerors, he relinquished his slaves to the governor and began a lifelong campaign for their freedom. He
returned to Spain to take up the fight at court, where his main
opponent was the influential theologian and historian Juan
Ginés de Sepúlveda. Sepúlveda had written "Concerning the
Just Cause of the War Against Indians," in which he argued
that Indians were "inferior to the Spaniards just as children
are to adults, women to men, and, indeed, one might even say,
as apes are to men." Las Casas's arguments won support at
court, but the harsh policies were already so ingrained in the
West Indies that there was little change in his lifetime. His
crusade to free the Indians from colonial rule inspired many
Latin American revolutionaries after him, including Simon
Bolívar (1783–1830), known as "the George Washington of
South America" because he freed six Latin American countries from Spanish rule.

The passage below is from *In Defense of the Indians*, las
Casas's direct response to Sepúlveda's arguments justifying
Spanish cruelty to the natives. It demonstrates the Renais-

Excerpted from *In Defense of the Indians*, by Bartolomé de las Casas, edited and translated
by Stafford Poole (DeKalb: Northern Illinois University Press, 1974). Copyright © 1974
by Northern Illinois University Press. Reprinted with permission.

sance humanist belief that people were not inferior or superior based on family lineage, but had certain unalienable rights that deserved respect and protection.

They who teach, either in word or in writing, that the natives of the New World, whom we commonly call Indians, ought to be conquered and subjugated by war before the gospel is proclaimed and preached to them so that, after they have finally been subjugated, they may be instructed and hear the word of God, make two disgraceful mistakes. First, in connection with divine and human law they abuse God's words and do violence to the Scriptures, to papal decrees, and to the teaching handed down from the holy fathers. And they go wrong again by quoting histories that are nothing but sheer fables and shameless nonsense. By means of these, men who are totally hostile to the poor Indians and who are their utterly deceitful enemies betray them. Second, they mistake the meaning of the decree or bull of the Supreme Pontiff Alexander VI, whose words they corrupt and twist in support of their opinions, as will be clear from all that follows.

Their error and ignorance are also convincingly substantiated by the fact that they draw conclusions on matters which concern a countless number of men and vast areas of extensive provinces. Since they do not fully understand all these things, it is the height of effrontery and rashness for them to attribute publicly to the Indians the gravest failings both of nature and conduct, condemning *en masse* [as a group] so many thousands of people, while, as a matter of fact, the greater number of them are free from these faults. All this drags innumerable souls to ruin and blocks the service of spreading the Christian religion by closing the eyes of those who, crazed by blind ambition, bend all their energies of mind and body to the one purpose of gaining wealth, power, honors, and dignities. For the sake of these things they kill and destroy with inhuman cruelty people who are completely innocent, meek, harmless, temperate, and quite ready and willing to receive and embrace the word of God.

Un-Christian Behavior Toward the Indians

Who is there possessed of only a sound mind, not to say a little knowledge of theology, who has dared to pronounce a judgment and opinion so un-Christian that it spawns so many cruel wars, so many massacres, so many bereavements, and so many deplorable evils? Do we not have Christ's words: "See that you never despise any of these little ones," "Alas for the man who provides obstacles," "He who is not with me is against me; and he who does not gather with me scatters," and "Each day has trouble enough of its own"? [Matthew 18:10 and 18:7. Luke 11:23. Matthew 6:34]. Who is so godless that he would want to incite men who are savage, ambitious, proud, greedy, uncontrolled, and everlastingly lazy to pillage their brothers and destroy their souls as well as their possessions, even though war is never lawful except when it is waged because of unavoidable necessity?

And so what man of sound mind will approve a war against men who are harmless, ignorant, gentle, temperate, unarmed, and destitute of every human defense? For the results of such a war are very surely the loss of the souls of that people who perish without knowing God and without the support of the sacraments, and, for the survivors, hatred and loathing of the Christian religion. Hence the purpose God intends, and for the attainment of which he suffered so much, may be frustrated by the evil and cruelty that our men wreak on them

Bartolomé de las Casas

with inhuman barbarity. What will these people think of Christ, the true God of the Christians, when they see Christians venting their rage against them with so many massacres, so much bloodshed without any just cause, at any rate without any just cause that they know of (nor can one even be imagined), and without any fault committed on their [the Indians] part against the Christians?

What good can come from these military campaigns that would, in the eyes of God, who evaluates all things with unutterable love, compensate for so many evils, so many injuries, and so many unaccustomed misfortunes? Furthermore, how will that nation love us, how will they become our friends (which is necessary if they are to accept our religion), when children see themselves deprived of parents, wives of husbands, and fathers of children and friends? When they see those they love wounded, imprisoned, plundered, and reduced from an immense number to a few? When they see their rulers stripped of their authority, crushed, and afflicted with a wretched slavery? All these things flow necessarily from war. Who is there who would want the gospel preached to himself in such a fashion? Does not this negative precept apply to all men in general: "See that you do not do to another what you would not have done to you by another"? [Tobit 2:16] And the same for the affirmative command: "So always treat others as you would like them to treat you." [Matthew 7:12] This is something that every man knows, grasps, and understands by the natural light that has been imparted to our minds.

An Unjust War

It is obvious from all this that they who teach that these gentlest of sheep must be tamed by ravening wolves in a savage war before they are to be fed with the word of God are wrong about matters that are totally clear and are opposed to the natural law. Moreover, they commit an ungodly error when they say that these wars are just if they are waged as they should be. They mean, I suppose, if they are waged with restraint, by killing only those who have to be killed in order to subjugate the rest. It is as if they held all the peoples of the New World shut up in cages or slave pens and would want to cut off as many human heads as are usually sold each day in the markets for the feeding and nourishment of the populace. (I suggest this as a comparison.) But if they would consider that war and the massacre of this timid race has lasted, not for one day or a hundred days, but for ten or twenty years, to the incredible harm of the natives; that, as they wander about, hidden and scattered through woods and forests, unarmed, naked, deprived of every human help, they are slaughtered by the Spaniards; that, stripped of their wealth and wretched, they are driven from their homes, stunned and frightened by the unbelievable terror with which their oppressors have filled them through the monstrous crimes they have committed. If those who say such things would only consider that the hearts of this unfortunate people are so shattered with fear that they want to hurl themselves headlong into the deepest caverns of the earth to escape the clutches of these plunderers, I have no doubt that they would say things that are more temperate and more wise.

The Dissolution of England's Parliament

Oliver Cromwell

Between 1642 and 1651, England was engaged in a bloody civil war, with supporters of King Charles I (also called Royalists or Cavaliers) battling supporters of Parliament (also called Parliamentarians or Roundheads). At issue was Charles's religious intolerance toward Protestants. Oliver Cromwell (1599–1658), himself a Calvinist and member of Parliament, became a general and led the Parliamentarians to victory. After Charles I was tried and executed in 1649, the monarchy was abolished and England was declared a republic known as "the Commonwealth." Cromwell became Lord Protector in 1653, establishing religious tolerance and raising England's prestige in Europe, which had been seriously declining since the death of Queen Elizabeth I (1533–1603). Despite his Parliamentarian origins, as Lord Protector, Cromwell's relationship with Parliament was rocky. He dissolved Parliament in 1653 for being corrupt, then again in 1655 for being uncooperative. An excerpt of his speech dissolving the 1655 Parliament is given below. Though it lacks the polish of a professional writer, nineteenth-century English historian Thomas Carlyle, who edited Cromwell's collected speeches and letters for publication, noted that "Practical Heroes, unfortunately, do not speak in blank verse."

Following this dissolution, a new Parliament was formed which offered to make Cromwell king. He refused the offer. He died of malaria in 1658. Two years later, the monarchy was restored in England under Charles II.

Excerpted from *The Letters and Speeches of Oliver Cromwell*, by Oliver Cromwell, edited by Thomas Carlyle (London: Methuen & Co., 1904).

G ENTLEMEN,
I perceive you are here as the House of Parliament,
by your Speaker whom I see here, and by your faces which
are in a great measure known to me. . . .

When I first met you in this room, it was to my apprehension the hopefullest day that ever mine eyes saw, as to
considerations of this world. For I did look at, as wrapt up in
you together with myself, the hopes and the happiness of,—
though not of the greatest,—yet a very great and the best
people in the world. And truly and unfeignedly I thought so:
as a people that have the highest and clearest profession
amongst them of the greatest glory, to wit Religion: as a
people that have been, like other nations, sometimes up and
sometimes down in our honour in the world, but yet never so
low but we might measure with other nations: and a people
that have had a stamp upon them from God . . . ; God having, as it were, summed up all our former honour and glory
in the things that are of glory to nations, in an epitome,
within these ten or twelve years last past! So that we knew
one another at home, and are well known abroad.

An Opportunity to Do Good

And if I be not very much mistaken, we were arrived,—as I,
and truly as I believe many others, did think,—at a very safe
port; where we might sit down and contemplate the dispen-
sations of God, and our mercies; and might know our mercies not to have been like to those of the ancients,—who did
make out their peace and prosperity, as they thought, by their
own endeavours; who could not say, as we, that all ours were
let down to us from God Himself; whose appearances and
providences amongst us are not to be outmatched by any
story. . . . Truly this was our condition. And I know nothing
else we had to do, save as Israel was commanded in that
most excellent Psalm of David: "The things which we have
heard and known, and our fathers have told us, we will not
hide them from their children; showing to the generation to
come the praise of the Lord, and His strength, and His wonderful works which He hath done. For He established a Tes-

timony in Jacob, and appointed a Law in Israel; which He commanded our fathers that they should make known to their children; that the generation to come might know them, even the children which should be born, who should arise and declare them to *their* children: that they might set their hope in God, and not forget the works of God, but keep His commandments." [Psalm 78:3–7]

This I thought had been a song and a work worthy of England, whereunto you might have happily invited them, had you had hearts unto it. You had this opportunity fairly delivered unto you. And if a history shall be written of these times and transactions, it will be said, it will not be denied, but that these things that I have spoken are true. . . . This talent was put into your hands. And I shall recur to that which I said at first: I came with very great joy and contentment and comfort, the first time I met you in this place. But we and these nations are, for the present, under some disappointment. If I had purposed to have played the orator, which I never did affect, nor do, nor I hope shall . . . , I doubt not upon easy suppositions, which I am persuaded every one among you will grant, we did meet upon such hopes as these.

A Second Chance Wasted

I met you a second time here: and I confess, at that meeting I had much abatement of my hopes; though not a total frustration. I confess that that which damped my hopes so soon was somewhat that did look like a parricide [the murder of one's parents]. It is obvious enough unto you that the management of affairs did savour of a not owning,—too-too much savour, I say, of a not owning of the authority that called you hither. But God left us not without an expedient that gave a second possibility—shall I say a possibility? it seemed to me a probability,—of recovering out of that dissatisfied condition we were all then in, towards some mutuality of satisfaction. And therefore by that Recognition . . . , suiting with the Indenture that returned you hither, to which afterwards also was added your own Declaration, conformable to, and in acceptance of, that expedient:—whereby, you had, though with a little check, another opportunity renewed unto you to have made this nation as happy as it could have been, if everything had smoothly run on from that first hour of your meeting. And indeed,—you will give me liberty of my thoughts and hopes,—I did think, as I have formerly found in that way that I have been engaged as a soldier, that some affronts put upon us, some disasters at the first, have made way for great and happy successes; and I did not at all despond but the stop put upon you would, in like manner, have made way for a blessing from God; that interruption being, as I thought, necessary to divert you from destructive and violent proceedings to give time for better deliberations; whereby leaving the Government as you found it, you might have proceeded to have made those good and wholesome laws which the people expected from you, and might have answered the grievances, and settled those other things proper to you as a Parliament: for which you would have had thanks from all that entrusted you. . . .

"I Have Not Once Heard from You"

What hath happened since that time I have not taken public notice of, as declining to intrench on Parliament privileges. For sure I am you will all bear me witness, that from your entering into the House upon the Recognition, to this very day, you have had no manner of interruption or hindrance of mine in proceeding to that blessed issue [that] the heart of a good man could propose to himself, to this very day. You see you have me very much locked up, as to what you have transacted among yourselves, from that time to this. . . . But something I shall take liberty to speak of to you.

As I may not take notice what you have been doing, so I think I have a very great liberty to tell you that I do not know what you been doing! . . . I do not know whether you have been alive or dead. I have not once heard from you all this time; I have not: and that you all know. If that be a fault that I have not, surely it hath not been mine! If I have had any melancholy thoughts, and have sat down by them, why might it not have been very lawful for me to think that

I was a person judged unconcerned in all these businesses?
I can assure you I have not 'so' reckoned myself; nor did I
reckon myself unconcerned in you. And so long as any just
patience could support my expectation, I would have waited
to the uttermost to have received from you the issues of your
consultations and resolutions. I have been careful of your
safety, and the safety of those that you represent, to whom
I reckon myself a servant.

But what messages have I disturbed you withal? What injury or indignity hath been done, or offered, either to your
persons or to any privileges of Parliament, since you sat? I
looked at myself as strictly obliged by my oath,—since your
recognising the Government in the authority of which you
were called hither and sat,—to give you all possible security, and to keep you from any unparliamentary interruption.
Think you I could not say more upon this subject, if I listed
to expatiate thereupon? But because my actions plead for
me, I shall say no more of this. . . . I say, I have been caring
for you, 'for' your quiet sitting; caring for your privileges,
as I said before, that they might not be interrupted; have
been seeking of God, from the great God, a blessing upon
you, and a blessing upon these nations. I have been consulting, if possibly I might in anything promote, in my
place, the real good of this Parliament, of the hopefulness
of which I have said so much unto you. And I did think it to
be my business rather to see the utmost issue, and what God
would produce by you, than unseasonably to intermeddle
with you. . . .

Discontent and Dissatisfaction

There be some trees that will not grow under the shadow of
other trees: There be some that choose,—a man may say so
by way of allusion,—to thrive under the shadow of other
trees. I will tell you what hath thriven, I will not say what
you have cherished, under your shadow; that were too hard.
Instead of peace and settlement, instead of mercy and truth
being brought together, righteousness and peace kissing
each other, by reconciling the honest people of these na-

tions, and settling the woful distempers that are amongst us;—which had been glorious things and worthy of Christians to have proposed,—weeds and nettles, briers and thorns, have thriven under your shadow! Dissettlement and division, discontent and dissatisfaction, together with real dangers to the whole, has been more multiplied within these five months of your sitting, than in some years before! Foundations have also been laid for the future renewing the troubles of these nations by all the enemies of them abroad and at home. Let not these words seem too sharp: for they are true as any mathematical demonstrations are, or can be. I say, the enemies of the peace of these nations abroad and at home, the discontented humours throughout these nations,—which I think no man will grudge to call by that name, or to make to allude to briers and thorns,—they have nourished themselves under your shadow! . . .

A Duty to God and the People

Now to speak a word or two to you of that I must profess in the name of the same Lord and wish that there had been no cause that I should have thus spoken to you! And though I have told you that I came with joy the first time; with some regret the second; yet now I speak with most regret at all! I look upon you as having among you many persons that I could lay down my life individually for. I could, through the grace of God, desire to lay down my life for you, so far am I from having an unkind or unchristian heart towards you in your particular capacities! I have that indeed as a work most incumbent upon me; I consulted what might be my duty in such a day as this; casting up all considerations. I must confess, as I told you, that I did think occasionally, this nation had suffered extremely in the respects mentioned; as also in the disappointments of their expectations of that justice which was due to them by your sitting thus long. And what have you brought forth? I did not nor cannot comprehend what it is. I would be loath to call it a Fate; that were too paganish a word. But there is something in it, that we have not our expectations. . . .

I have troubled you with a long Speech; and I believe it may not have the same resentment [sensation] with all that it hath with some. But because that is unknown to me, I shall leave it to God; and conclude with that: that I think myself bound,—in my duty to God and the people of these nations, to their safety and good in every respect,—I think it my duty to tell you that it is not for the profit of these nations, nor fit for the common and public good, for you to continue here any longer. And therefore I do declare unto you, That I do dissolve this Parliament.

Chapter 3

Religion and Philosophy

Chapter Preface

D uring the Middle Ages in Europe, philosophical study
was restricted to the monasteries, where it was rigidly
controlled by the Holy Roman Church. The basic teachings
that emerged from these strict confines focused on how
people should quietly accept their lot in life, no matter how
seemingly awful or unfair, so that they could concentrate on
their spiritual growth. Life on earth was described as a kind
of hell to be endured so that people might later enjoy their
heavenly rewards.

Two events started the changes that would soon sweep
aside this medieval way of thinking. First, the introduction
of the printing press in 1451 made new philosophies about
the world, as well as criticisms of the old philosophies,
available to a larger audience. Second, in 1453 Muslims expelled Greek scholars from Constantinople who brought the
classical Greek texts with them to Europe. These texts, including those of Greek philosopher Plato (427?–347 B.C.),
which had been suppressed by the Roman Catholic Church,
sparked a renewed interest in the culture and teachings of
ancient Rome and Greece. European thinkers, weary of the
dour demands of the church as well as its rampant corruption, anxiously embraced the old texts, which focused not
on the afterlife, but on how to best live this life.

This new philosophy of "humanism" celebrated the human spirit in all its strengths and weaknesses. Instead of being thought of as insignificant cogs in a universal plan, humans were now considered embodiments of God's goodness.
Individual free will was stressed, and people were encouraged to seek the limits of their talent and ambition rather than
accept a fate dictated by birth into a particular social class.

The church, which greatly influenced monarchs across
Europe, felt the impact of this new philosophy. First, En-

gland's King Henry VIII pulled away and began his own Anglican Church. Second, clergyman Martin Luther, outraged by church hypocrisies, also turned away to found Protestantism. In response to these major events, from around 1550 the Roman Church began a series of spiritual and institutional reforms known as the Reformation by Catholics and the Counter-Reformation by Protestants.

The Ascent of Mont Ventoux

Francesco Petrarch

Italian scholar, poet, and philosopher Francesco Petrarch (1304–1374) is considered the first person to effectively close the door on the Middle Ages and open a new one onto the Renaissance. He is often described as the first Renaissance Man, not only because he was the master of many disciplines, but because he rejected the rigid artistic and moral dogmatism of the Middle Ages. Instead, he proposed a Humanist philosophy, one centered around people's free will and unquenchable thirst for self-knowledge. He was not a philosopher in the traditional sense of creating a new model for seeing the world. He was more a moral philosopher in that he emphasized the art of living well and happily. Although he had little effect on the political or economic world, he had enormous influence in shaping the artistic and moral sensibilities that characterized the Renaissance. The greatest thinkers of the age, from artist-scientist Leonardo da Vinci (1452–1519) to astronomer Galileo Galilei (1564–1642) were in some way influenced by Petrarch.

"The Ascent of Mont Ventoux," excerpted below, is hailed as one of Petrarch's literary masterpieces. Addressed to his former professor of theology, Francesco Dionigi de'Roberti (c. 1285–1342), the letter describes Petrarch's climb in 1336 of a relatively high mountain near where he was raised as a boy. Even though he appears to be vividly relating his climbing experience, he is in fact presenting an allegory of his personal "climb" to a higher state of consciousness.

Today I ascended the highest mountain in this region, which, not without cause, they call the Windy Peak. Nothing but the desire to see its conspicuous height was the reason for this undertaking. For many years I have been intending to make this expedition. You know that since my early childhood, as fate tossed around human affairs, I have been tossed around in these parts, and this mountain, visible far and wide from everywhere, is always in your view. So I was at last seized by the impulse to accomplish what I had always wanted to do. . . .

[My brother and I] left home on the appointed day and arrived at Malaucène at night. This is a place at the northern foot of the mountain. We spent a day there and began our ascent this morning, each of us accompanied by a single servant. From the start we encountered a good deal of trouble, for the mountain is a steep and almost inaccessible pile of rocky material. However, what the Poet [first-century B.C. Roman poet Publius Vergilius Maro (Virgil)] says is appropriate: "Ruthless striving overcomes everything."

Difficulties of the Climb

The day was long, the air was mild; this and vigorous minds, strong and supple bodies, and all the other conditions assisted us on our way. The only obstacle was the nature of the spot. We found an aged shepherd in the folds of the mountain who tried with many words to dissuade us from the ascent. He said he had been up to the highest summit in just such youthful fervor fifty years ago and had brought home nothing but regret and pains, and his body as well as his clothes torn by rocks and thorny underbrush. Never before and never since had the people there heard of any man who dared a similar feat. While he was shouting these words at us, our desire increased just because of his warnings; for young people's minds do not give credence to advisers. When the old man saw that he was exerting himself in vain, he went with us a little way forward through the rocks and pointed with his finger to a steep path. He gave us much good advice and repeated it again and again at our backs when we were already at quite a distance. We left with him whatever of our clothes and other belongings might encumber us, intent only on the ascent, and began to climb with merry alacrity. However, as almost always happens, the daring attempt was soon followed by quick fatigue.

Not far from our start we stopped at a rock. From there we went on again, proceeding at a slower pace, to be sure. I in particular made my way up with considerably more modest steps. My brother endeavored to reach the summit by the very ridge of the mountain on a short cut; I, being so much more of a weakling, was bending down toward the valley. When he called me back and showed me the better way, I answered that I hoped to find an easier access on the other side and was not afraid of a longer route on which I might proceed more smoothly. With such an excuse I tried to palliate my laziness, and, when the others had already reached the higher zones, I was still wandering through the valleys, where no more comfortable access was revealed, while the way became longer and longer and the vain fatigue grew heavier and heavier. At last I felt utterly disgusted, began to regret my perplexing error, and decided to attempt the heights with a wholehearted effort. Weary and exhausted, I reached my brother, who had been waiting for me and was refreshed by a good long rest. For a while we went on together at the same pace. However, hardly had we left that rock behind us when I forgot the detour I had made just a short while before and was once more drawing down the lower regions. Again I wandered through the valleys, looking for the longer and easier path and stumbling only into longer difficulties. Thus I indeed put off the disagreeable strain of climbing.

Lessons from the Climb

But nature is not overcome by man's devices; a corporeal thing cannot reach the heights by descending. What shall I say? My brother laughed at me; I was indignant; this happened to me three times and more within a few hours. So often was I frustrated in my hopes that at last I sat down in a valley. There I leaped in my winged thoughts from things corporeal to what is incorporeal and addressed myself in words like these:

"What you have so often experienced today while climbing this mountain happens to you, you must know, and to many others who are making their way toward the blessed life. This is not easily understood by us men, because the motions of the body lie open, while those of the mind are invisible and hidden. The life we call blessed is located on a high peak. 'A narrow way,'[Matthew 7:14] they say, leads up to it. Many hilltops intervene, and we must proceed 'from virtue to virtue' with exalted steps. On the highest summit is set the end of all, the goal toward which our pilgrimage is directed. Every man wants to arrive there. However, as [first-century B.C. Roman poet Publius Ovidius (Ovid)] Naso says: 'Wanting is not enough; long and you attain it.' You certainly do not merely want; you have a longing, unless you are deceiving yourself in this respect as in so many others. What is it, then, that keeps you back? Evidently nothing but the smoother way that leads through the meanest earthly pleasures and looks easier at first sight. However, having strayed far in error, you must either ascend to the summit of the blessed life under the heavy burden of hard striving, ill deferred, or lie prostrate in your slothfulness in the valleys of your sins. If 'darkness and the shadow of death' [Psalms 106(107):10; Job 34:22] find you there—I shudder while I pronounce these ominous words—you must pass the eternal night in incessant torments."

You cannot imagine how much comfort this thought brought my mind and body for what lay still ahead of me. Would that I might achieve with my mind the journey for which I am longing day and night as I achieved with the feet of my body my journey today after overcoming all obstacles. And I wonder whether it ought not to be much easier to accomplish what can be done by means of the agile and immortal mind without any local motion "in the twinkling of the trembling eye" [I Corinthians 15:52] than what is to be performed in the succession of time by the service of the frail body that is doomed to die and under the heavy load of the limbs.

There is a summit, higher than all the others. The people in the woods up there call it "Sonny," I do not know why. However, I suspect they use the word in a sense opposite to its meaning, as is done sometimes in other cases too. For it really looks like the father of all the surrounding mountains. On its top is a small level stretch. There at last we rested from our fatigue.

Finding His Place in the World

And now, my dear father, since you have heard what sorrows arose in my breast during my climb, listen also to what remains to be told. Devote, I beseech you, one of your hours to reading what I did during one of my days. At first I stood there almost benumbed, overwhelmed by a gale such as I had never felt before and by the unusually open and wide view. I looked around me: clouds were gathering below my feet, and Athos [mountain in northern Greece] and Olympus [mountain in northeast Greece, where Greek mythology claims the gods lived] grew less incredible, since I saw on a mountain of lesser fame what I had heard and read about them. . . .

Then another thought took possession of my mind, leading it from the contemplation of space to that of time, and I said to myself: "This day marks the completion of the tenth year since you gave up the studies of your boyhood and left Bologna. O immortal God, O immutable Wisdom! How many and how great were the changes you have had to undergo in your moral habits since then." I will not speak of what is still left undone, for I am not yet in port that I might think in security of the storms I have had to endure. The time will perhaps come when I can review all this in the order in which it happened, using as a prologue that passage of your favorite [in fifth-century theologian Saint] Augustine: "Let me remember my past mean acts and the carnal corruption of my soul, not that I love them, but that I may love Thee, my God." [in *Confessions* ii, I. 1]

Many dubious and troublesome things are still in store for me. What I used to love, I love no longer. But I lie: I love it still, but less passionately. Again have I lied: I love it, but more timidly, more sadly. Now at last I have told the truth; for thus it is: I love, but what I should love not to love, what I should wish to hate. Nevertheless I love it, but against my will, under compulsion and in sorrow and mourning. To my own misfortune I experience in myself now the meaning of that most famous line: "Hate I shall, if I can; if I can't, I shall love though not willing" [in Ovid's *Amores* iii.II.35]. The third year has not yet elapsed since that perverted and malicious will, which had totally seized me and reigned in the court of my heart without an opponent, began to encounter a rebel offering resistance. A stubborn and still undecided battle has been long raging on the field of my thoughts for the supremacy of one of the two men within me [his internal struggle between passions of the flesh and his desire for spiritual development].

Thus I revolved in my thoughts the history of the last decade. Then I dismissed my sorrow at the past and asked myself: "Suppose you succeed in protracting this rapidly fleeing life for another decade, and come as much nearer to virtue, in proportion to the span of time, as you have been freed from your former obstinacy during these last two years as a result of the struggle of the new and the old wills— would you then not be able—perhaps not with certainty but with reasonable hope at least—to meet death in your fortieth year with equal mind and cease to care for that remnant of life which descends into old age?"

These and like considerations rose in my breast again and again, dear father. I was glad of the progress I had made, but I wept over my imperfection and was grieved by the fickleness of all that men do. In this manner I seemed to have somehow forgotten the place I had come to and why, until I was warned to throw off such sorrows, for which another place would be more appropriate. I had better look around and see what I had intended to see in coming here. The time to leave was approaching, they said. The sun was already setting, and the shadow of the mountain was growing longer and longer. Like a man aroused from sleep, I turned back and looked toward the west. . . .

How often, do you think, did I turn back and look up to the summit of the mountain today while I was walking down? It seemed to me hardly higher than a cubit compared to the height of human contemplation, were the latter not plunged into the filth of earthly sordidness. This too occurred to me at every step: "If you do not regret undergoing so much sweat and hard labor to lift the body a bit nearer to heaven, ought any cross or jail or torture to frighten the mind that is trying to come nearer to God and set its feet upon the swollen summit of insolence and upon the fate of mortal men?" And this too: "How few will ever succeed in not diverging from this path because of fear of hardship or desire for smooth comfort?". . .

Such emotions were rousing a storm in my breast as, without perceiving the roughness of the path, I returned late at night to the little rustic inn from which I had set out before dawn. The moon was shining all night long and offered her friendly service to the wanderers. While the servants were busy preparing our meal, I withdrew quite alone into a remote part of the house to write this letter to you in all haste and on the spur of the moment. I was afraid the intention to write might evaporate, since the rapid change of scene was likely to cause a change of mood if I deferred it.

And thus, most loving father, gather from this letter how eager I am to leave nothing whatever in my heart hidden from your eyes. Not only do I lay my whole life open to you with the utmost care but every single thought of mine. Pray for these thoughts, I beseech you, that they may at last find stability. So long have they been idling about and, finding no firm stand, been uselessly driven through so many matters. May they now turn at last to the One, the Good, the True, the stably Abiding.

Farewell.

On the twenty-sixth day of April, at Malaucène.

A Protest Against the Sale of Indulgences

Martin Luther

> Few people have changed the world as drastically as did
> Martin Luther (1483–1546). A German monk and scholar at
> the University of Wittenberg, Luther is the acknowledged
> founder of Lutheranism and, along with his friend, theolo-
> gian and educator Philipp Melanchthon (1497–1560), of
> Protestantism. Luther's rebellion against the Catholic Church
> was not aimed at its authority, but at the corruption of certain
> principles. In keeping with the Renaissance's emphasis on
> Humanism and personal growth, Luther argued that individu-
> als had a personal relationship with God and did not need an
> intermediary such as the church to enhance or interpret that
> relationship.
>
> The following letter by Luther to his archbishop explains
> one of his major contentions with the church, the sale of
> indulgences. Originally, indulgences were sums of money a
> penitent could pay as part of an act of contrition to be
> absolved of a sin. But the custom became corrupted when the
> church modified it to include a sum to be paid to reduce one's
> time in purgatory. Huge amounts of money were amassed,
> which added to the personal wealth of many involved in
> administering indulgences.

To the Most Reverend Father in Christ, the most Illustrious Lord, Baron Albert, Archbishop and Primate of the
Churches of Magdeburg and Mainz, Marquis of Branden-

Excerpted from *Reformation Writings of Martin Luther, vol. I: The Basis of the Protestant,* by Martin Luther, edited and translated by Bertram Lee Woolf (London: Lutterworth
Press, 1952). Copyright © 1952 by Lutterworth Press. Reprinted with permission.

burg, etc., my own Superior and Pastor in Christ, held in all due honour and respect, most gracious.

Jesus[1]

May God give you all the grace and mercy that exist, most reverend Father in Christ, and most illustrious Prince. Pardon me, if I, a man of no standing, should yet have the temerity to think of writing to your Sublime Excellency. The Lord Jesus is my witness that I am well aware that I am of mean condition and no consequence; and I have therefore long deferred doing what I am now making bold to do. Above all else, I am urged by my duty of loyalty to you, a duty which I acknowledge I owe you, my most Reverend Father in Christ. Perhaps then, your Excellency will deign to look on me who am but dust, and, of your episcopal clemency, give heed to my request.

False Promises of Salvation

Papal indulgences for building St. Peter's are being carried round under the authority of your most distinguished self. The purpose of the protest I am now making is not concerned with the substance of the message which the preachers proclaim so loudly; for I have not myself actually heard them; but I do deplore the very mistaken impressions which the common people have gained, and which are universally current among the masses. For example, the poor souls believe that if they buy these letters of indulgence, their own salvation is assured. Again, that souls are liberated from purgatory at the very moment that contributions are cast into the chest. Further, that these indulgences are of so effective a grace that there is no sin too great to be wiped out by them, even if, as they say, *per impossible,* it consisted in having violated the mother of God. Again, that these indulgences free a man from all punishment and guilt. God have mercy on us! That is how those committed to your care, good Father, are taught to regard death. It will be very hard for you to render your account for them all, and it will grow

---

1. It was Luther's custom to invoke the name of Jesus before beginning to write.

still harder. That is why I have not been able to keep silence any longer about these things. For no man is assured of salvation by a gift, be it conferred by a bishop, since such an assurance is not given even by the infused grace of God; rather the Apostle bids us always to work out our salvation in fear and trembling [Philippians 2:12], and, we read, "the righteous shall scarcely be saved" [I Peter 4:18]. Moreover, so narrow is the way that leads to life [Matthew 7:14] that the Lord, speaking through the prophets Amos [Matthew 4:11] and Zechariah [Matthew 3:2], calls those who shall be saved "brands plucked from the burning". Indeed the Lord points everywhere to the difficulty of being saved. Why then do the preachers utter those falsehoods, and give promises of pardons, and make the people feel safe and unafraid? At no time do indulgences give anything advantageous to the salvation or sanctity of the soul; at best they only do away with the external punishments, which it has hitherto been the custom to impose according to canon law.

Moreover, works of piety and love are infinitely preferable to indulgences. Yet it is not of these that they preach with great pomp and authority; rather, they pass these works over in silence, in order to proclaim the indulgences. Nevertheless, the prime and sole duty of all bishops is to teach the people the gospel and the love of Christ. Christ nowhere commands the preaching of indulgences, but He insistently commands that the gospel should be preached. Then what a dreadful thing it is, and how great the peril of a bishop, who says nothing about the gospel, but readily allows indulgences to be noised abroad among his people in preference to the gospel! Will not Christ say to him, "You are straining at a gnat and swallowing a camel"? [Matthew 23:24]

Bringing Disrepute to Your Illustrious Sublimity

In addition, there is this fact, Most Reverend Father in the Lord, that an "Instruction" to the sub-commissioners has been issued in your name, Reverend Father, but surely without the knowledge and consent of your Fatherly Reverence.

This "Instruction" declares that one of the chief graces of these indulgences is God's incalculable gift, whereby a man is reconciled to God, and all the pains of purgatory are abolished; also, that there is no need for contrite hearts on the part of those who pay for souls to be redeemed from purga-

Ninety-Five Theses

Frustrated at the lack of reaction to his suggestions for reform, in 1513 Martin Luther wrote down his famous "Ninety-Five Theses," detailing his complaints against the Catholic Church, which he then attached to the door of All Saints Church in Wittenberg. His theses, as excerpted below, emphasize that salvation comes through faith alone and that each Christian has a personal relationship with God that does not require intervention from a priest. The Vatican saw this as an attack on papal authority and excommunicated Luther in 1520. Luther answered by burning the writ of excommunication.

Out of love and zeal for truth and the desire to bring it to light, the following theses will be publicly discussed at Wittenberg under the chairmanship of the reverend father Martin Lutther [Luther spelled his name Lutther in this preamble], Master of Arts and Sacred Theology and regularly appointed Lecturer on these subjects at that place. He requests that those who cannot be present to debate orally with us will do so by letter.

In the Name of Our Lord Jesus Christ. Amen.

1. When our Lord and Master Jesus Christ said, "Repent" [Matt. 4:17], he willed the entire life of believers to be one of repentance.

2. This word cannot be understood as referring to the sacrament of penance, that is, confession and satisfaction, as administered by the clergy.

3. Yet it does not mean solely inner repentance; such inner repentance is worthless unless it produces various outward mortifications of the flesh. . . .

14. Imperfect piety or love on the part of the dying per-

tory, or who buy the tickets of indulgence.

What am I to do, best of primates [archbishops] and most illustrious of princes, except pray your Most Fatherly Reverence in the name of Jesus Christ to deign to give your paternal attention to this matter, and totally withdraw those

son necessarily brings with it great fear; and the smaller the love, the greater the fear.

15. This fear or horror is sufficient in itself, to say nothing of other things, to constitute the penalty of purgatory, since it is very near the horror of despair.

16. Hell, purgatory, and heaven seem to differ the same as despair, fear, and assurance of salvation.

17. It seems as though for the souls in purgatory fear should necessarily decrease and love increase.

18. Furthermore, it does not seem proved, either by reason or Scripture, that souls in purgatory are outside the state of merit, that is, unable to grow in love.

19. Nor does it seem proved that souls in purgatory, at least not all of them, are certain and assured of their own salvation, even if we ourselves may be entirely certain of it.

20. Therefore the pope, when he uses the words "plenary remission of all penalties," does not actually mean "all penalties," but only those imposed by himself.

21. Thus those indulgence preachers are in error who say that a man is absolved from every penalty and saved by papal indulgences.

22. As a matter of fact, the pope remits to souls in purgatory no penalty which, according to canon law, they should have paid in this life.

23. If remission of all penalties whatsoever could be granted to anyone at all, certainly it would be granted only to the most perfect, that is, to very few.

24. For this reason most people are necessarily deceived by that indiscriminate and high-sounding promise of release from penalty.

Martin Luther, *Luther's Work*. Harold J. Grim, ed. Philadelphia: Muhlenberg Press, 1957.

summary instructions altogether, and order the indulgence preachers to adopt another style of preaching. Otherwise, it may happen that someone will arise, publish his own summary instructions, and confute those preachers and the present instructions. This will bring your Most Illustrious Sublimity into the greatest disrepute, an event which I should heartily detest; yet I fear that it will happen unless appropriate steps are taken immediately.

I beg your Most Illustrious Grace to accept my humble and dutiful respects in the manner of a prince and a bishop: with the utmost clemency, since I put them forward in good faith, and I am entirely devoted to your Most Fatherly Reverence; and because I am also a member of your flock. May the Lord Jesus guard your Most Fatherly Reverence for ever. Amen.

Wittenberg, 1517. Eve of All Saints. If it please your Fatherly Reverence, you may glance at the theses of mine enclosed herewith, and see how dubious is the question of indulgences, although these people are broadcasting them as if it were most indubitable.

Your unworthy son,
Martin Luther,
Augustinian, Doctor of Sacred Theology.

Human Nature and Free Will

John Calvin

French theologian John Calvin (1509–1564) converted to Protestantism at a time when the French government severely persecuted anyone who was not Catholic. This courage of his convictions led Calvin to become a leading figure in Protestantism, causing him to sometimes be referred to as "the Protestant Pope." His austere approach to Christianity resulted in the founding of the morally strict Puritans, who sought to "purify" the Church of England from any remnants of the Catholic Church, and of Calvinism, a religion begun by his followers after his death.

Calvin's major work was the *Institutes of the Christian Religion* (1536), excerpted below, the first systematic explanation of Protestant doctrine. Widely translated, it became the most influential religious manual of the sixteenth-century Reformation, when the rise of Protestantism split the Roman Catholic Church.

I. *Man proceeded spotless from God's hand; therefore he may not shift the blame for his sins to the Creator*

We must now speak of the creation of man: not only because among all God's works here is the noblest and most remarkable example of his justice, wisdom, and goodness; but because, as we said at the beginning, we cannot have a clear and complete knowledge of God unless it is accompanied by a corresponding knowledge of ourselves. This knowledge of ourselves is twofold: namely, to know what we were like when we were first created and what our condition became after the fall of Adam. While it would be of little benefit to understand our creation unless we recognized in this sad ruin what our nature in its corruption and deformity is like, we shall nevertheless be content for the moment with the description of our originally upright nature. And to be sure, before we come to the miserable condition of man to which he is now subjected, it is worth-while to know what he was like when first created. Now we must guard against singling out only those natural evils of man, lest we seem to attribute them to the Author of nature. For in this excuse, impiety thinks it has sufficient defense, if it is able to claim that whatever defects it possesses have in some way proceeded from God. It does not hesitate, if it is reproved, to contend with God himself, and to impute to him the fault of which it is deservedly accused. And those who wish to seem to speak more reverently of the Godhead still willingly blame their depravity on nature, not realizing that they also, although more obscurely, insult God. For if any defect were proved to inhere in nature, this would bring reproach upon him.

Since, then, we see the flesh panting for every subterfuge by which it thinks that the blame for its own evils may in any way be diverted from itself to another, we must diligently oppose this evil intent. Therefore we must so deal with the calamity of mankind that we may cut off every shift, and may vindicate God's justice from every accusation. Afterward, in the proper place, we shall see how far away men are from the purity that was bestowed upon Adam. And first we must realize that when he was taken from earth and clay [Gen. 2:7; 18:27], his pride was bridled. For nothing is more absurd than for those who not only "dwell in houses of clay" [Job 4:19], but who are themselves in part earth and dust, to boast of their own excellence. But since God not only deigned to give life to an earthen vessel, but also willed it to be the abode of an immortal spirit, Adam could rightly glory in the great liberality of his Maker. . . .

7. Understanding and will as the truly fundamental faculties

. . . [L]et us, therefore, hold—as indeed is suitable to our present purpose—that the human soul consists of two faculties, understanding and will. Let the office, moreover, of understanding be to distinguish between objects, as each seems worthy of approval or disapproval; while that of the will, to choose and follow what the understanding pronounces good, but to reject and flee what it disapproves. Let not those minutiae of [fourth-century B.C. Greek philosopher] Aristotle delay us here, that the mind has no motion in itself, but is moved by choice. This choice he calls the appetitive understanding. Not to entangle ourselves in useless questions, let it be enough for us that the understanding is, as it were, the leader and governor of the soul; and that the will is always mindful of the bidding of the understanding, and in its own desires awaits the judgment of the understanding. For this reason, Aristotle himself truly teaches the same: that shunning or seeking out in the appetite corresponds to affirming or denying in the mind. Indeed, in another place we shall see how firmly the understanding now governs the direction of the will; here we wish to say only this, that no power can be found in the soul that does not duly have reference to one or the other of these members. And in this way we include sense under understanding. The philosophers, on the other hand, make this distinction: that sense inclines to pleasure, while understanding follows the good; thence it comes about that sensual appetite becomes inordinate desire and lust; the inclination of the understanding, will. Again, for the term "appetite," which they prefer, I substitute the word "will," which is more common.

8. Free choice and Adam's responsibility

Therefore God provided man's soul with a mind, by which to distinguish good from evil, right from wrong; and, with the light of reason as guide, to distinguish what should be followed from what should be avoided. . . . To this he joined the will, under whose control is choice. Man in his first condition excelled in these pre-eminent endowments, so that his reason, understanding, prudence, and judgment not only sufficed for the direction of his earthly life, but by them men mounted up even to God and eternal bliss. Then was choice added, to direct the appetites and control all the organic motions, and thus make the will completely amenable to the guidance of the reason.

In this integrity man by free will had the power, if he so willed, to attain eternal life. Here it would be out of place to raise the question of God's secret predestination because our present subject is not what can happen or not, but what man's nature was like. Therefore Adam could have stood if he wished, seeing that he fell solely by his own will. But it was because his will was capable of being bent to one side or the other, and was not given the constancy to persevere, that he fell so easily. Yet his choice of good and evil was free, and not that alone, but the highest rectitude was in his mind and will, and all the organic parts were rightly composed to obedience, until in destroying himself he corrupted his own blessings.

Hence the great obscurity faced by the philosophers, for they were seeking in a ruin for a building, and in scattered fragments for a well-knit structure. They held this principle, that man would not be a rational animal unless he possessed free choice of good and evil; also it entered their minds that the distinction between virtues and vices would be obliterated if man did not order his life by his own planning. Well reasoned so far—if there had been no change in man. But since this was hidden from them, it is no wonder they mix up heaven and earth! They, as professed disciples of Christ, are obviously playing the fool when, by compromising between the opinions of the philosophers and heavenly doctrine, so that these touch neither heaven nor earth, in man—who is lost and sunk down into spiritual destruction—they still seek after free choice. But these matters will be better dealt with in their proper place. Now we need bear only this in mind: man was far different at the first creation from his whole posterity, who, deriving their origin from him in his corrupted state, have contracted from him a hereditary taint. For, the individual parts of his soul were formed to uprightness, the soundness of his mind stood firm, and his will was free to choose the good. If anyone objects that his will was placed in an insecure position because its power was weak, his status should have availed to remove any excuse; nor was it reasonable for God to be constrained by the necessity of making a man who either could not or would not sin at all. Such a nature would, indeed, have been more excellent. But to quarrel with God on this precise point, as if he ought to have conferred this upon man, is more than iniquitous [unjust], inasmuch as it was in his own choice to give whatever he pleased. But the reason he did not sustain man by the virtue of perseverance lies hidden in his plan; sobriety is for us the part of wisdom. Man, indeed, received the ability provided he exercised the will; but he did not have the will to use his ability, for this exercising of the will would have been followed by perseverance. Yet he is not excusable, for he received so much that he voluntarily brought about his own destruction; indeed, no necessity was imposed upon God of giving man other than a mediocre and even transitory will, that from man's Fall he might gather occasion for his own glory.

Concerning the Things of Which We May Doubt

René Descartes

French mathematician and philosopher René Descartes (1596–1650) is considered by many to be the founder of modern philosophy. With his famous pronouncement, "I think, therefore I am," he broke from the medieval Scholastic tradition of philosophy, which interpreted everything through a classically Christian point of view. Although Descartes remained a devout Catholic his entire life, he adopted the Renaissance spirit of seeking truth for its own sake, regardless of the consequences on traditional beliefs.

Descartes' first work, *The World*, was nearly completed in 1633, when he heard that Italian astronomer Galileo Galilei (1564–1642) had been condemned as a heretic by the Vatican for endorsing Nicolaus Copernicus's (1473–1543) theory that the Earth was not the center of the universe. Descartes quietly withdrew efforts to publish his work, which also supported Copernicus. His most famous work, *Discourse on Method* (1637), begins with the notion to never accept anything as true that you did not personally see or experience. The following passage from *Meditations on First Philosophy* (1640) further explores his rejection of conventional wisdom and encouragement toward experimentation that inspired many subsequent philosophers, mathematicians, and scientists. However, though publication of *Meditations* confirmed his position as a respected philosopher, it also brought accusations of atheism, resulting in his works being added to the *Index*, the list of books forbidden by the Catholic Church.

It is now several years since I first became aware how many false opinions I had from my childhood been admitting as true, and how doubtful was everything I have subsequently based on them. Accordingly I have ever since been convinced that if I am to establish anything firm and lasting in the sciences, I must once for all, and by a deliberate effort, rid myself of all those opinions to which I have hitherto given credence, starting entirely anew, and building from the foundations up. But as this enterprise was evidently one of great magnitude, I waited until I had attained an age so mature that I could no longer expect that I should at any later date be better able to execute my design. This is what has made me delay so long; and I should now be failing in my duty, were I to continue consuming in deliberation such time for action as still remains to me.

Today, then, as I have suitably freed my mind from all cares, and have secured for myself an assured leisure in peaceful solitude, I shall at last apply myself earnestly and freely to the general overthrow of all my former opinions. In doing so, it will not be necessary for me to show that they are one and all false; that is perhaps more than can be done. But since reason has already persuaded me that I ought to withhold belief no less carefully from things not entirely certain and indubitable than from those which appear to me manifestly false, I shall be justified in setting all of them aside, if in each case I can find any ground whatsoever for regarding them as dubitable. Nor in so doing shall I be investigating each belief separately—that, like inquiry into their falsity, would be an endless labor. The withdrawal of foundations involves the downfall of whatever rests on these foundations, and what I shall therefore begin by examining are the principles on which my former beliefs rested.

Whatever, up to the present, I have accepted as possessed of the highest truth and certainty I have learned either from the senses or through the senses. Now these senses I have sometimes found to be deceptive; and it is only prudent never to place complete confidence in that by which we have even once been deceived.

But, it may be said, although the senses sometimes deceive us regarding minute objects, or such as are at a great distance from us, there are yet many other things which, though known by way of sense, are too evident to be doubted; as, for instance, that I am in this place, seated by the fire, attired in a dressing-gown, having this paper in my hands, and other similar seeming certainties. Can I deny that these hands and this body are mine, save perhaps by comparing myself to those who are insane, and whose brains are so disturbed and clouded by dark bilious vapors that they persist in assuring us that they are kings, when in fact they are in extreme poverty; or that they are clothed in gold and purple when they are in fact destitute of any covering; or that their head is made of clay and their body of glass, or that they are pumpkins. They are mad; and I should be no less insane were I to follow examples so extravagant.

None the less I must bear in mind that I am a man, and am therefore in the habit of sleeping, and that what the insane represent to themselves in their waking moments I represent to myself, with other things even less probable, in my dreams. How often, indeed, have I dreamt of myself being in this place, dressed and seated by the fire, whilst all the time I was lying undressed in bed! At the present moment it certainly seems that in looking at this paper I do so with open eyes, that the head which I move is not asleep, that it is deliberately and of set purpose that I extend this hand, and that I am sensing the hand. The things which happen to the sleeper are not so clear nor so distinct as all of these are. I cannot, however, but remind myself that on many occasions I have in sleep been deceived by similar illusions; and on more careful study of them I see that there are no certain marks distinguishing waking from sleep; and I see this so manifestly that, lost in amazement, I am almost persuaded that I am now dreaming.

Let us, then, suppose ourselves to be asleep, and that all these particulars—namely, that we open our eyes, move the head, extend the hands—are false and illusory; and let us reflect that our hands perhaps, and the whole body, are not what we see them as being. Nevertheless we must at least agree that the things seen by us in sleep are as it were like painted images, and cannot have been formed save in the likeness of what is real and true. The types of things depicted, eyes, head, hands, etc.—these at least are not imaginary, but true and existent. For in truth when painters endeavor with all possible artifice to represent sirens and satyrs by forms the most fantastic and unusual, they cannot assign them natures which are entirely new, but only make a certain selection of limbs from different animals. Even should they excogitate something so novel that nothing similar has ever before been seen, and that their work represents to us a thing entirely fictitious and false, the colors used in depicting them cannot be similarly fictitious; they at least must truly exist. And by this same reasoning, even should those general things, viz., a body, eyes, a head, hands and such like, be imaginary, we are yet bound to admit that there are things simpler and more universal which are real existents and by the intermixture of which, as in the case of the colors, all the images of things of which we have any awareness be they true and real or false and fantastic, are formed. To this class of things belong corporeal nature in general and its extension, the shape of extended things, their quantity or magnitude, and their number, as also the location in which they are, the time through which they endure, and other similar things.

This, perhaps, is why we not unreasonably conclude that physics, astronomy, medicine, and all other disciplines treating of composite things are of doubtful character, and that arithmetic, geometry, etc., treating only of the simplest and most general things and but little concerned as to whether or not they are actual existents, have a content that is certain and indubitable. For whether I am awake or dreaming, 2 and 3 are 5, a square has no more than four sides; and it does not seem possible that truths so evident can ever be suspected of falsity.

Proving God Exists

Yet even these truths can be questioned. That God exists, that He is all-powerful and has created me such as I am, has long been my settled opinion. How, then, do I know that He has not arranged that there be no Earth, no heavens, no extended thing, no shape, no magnitude, no location, while at the same time securing that all these things appear to me to exist precisely as they now do? Others, as I sometimes think, deceive themselves in the things which they believe they know best. How do I know that I am not myself deceived every time I add 2 and 3, or count the sides of a square, or judge of things yet simpler, if anything simpler can be suggested? But perhaps God has not been willing that I should be thus deceived, for He is said to be supremely good. If, however, it be repugnant to the goodness of God to have created me such that I am constantly subject to deception, it would also appear to be contrary to His goodness to permit me to be sometimes deceived, and that He does permit this is not in doubt.

There may be those who might prefer to deny the existence of a God so powerful, rather than to believe that all other things are uncertain. Let us, for the present, not oppose them; let us allow, in the manner of their view, that all which has been said regarding God is a fable. Even so we shall not have met and answered the doubts suggested above regarding the reliability of our mental faculties; instead we shall have given added force to them. For in whatever way it be supposed that I have come to be what I am, whether by fate or by chance, or by a continual succession and connection of things, or by some other means, since to be deceived and to err is an imperfection, the likelihood of my being so imperfect as to be the constant victim of deception will be increased in proportion as the power to which they assign my origin is lessened. To such argument I have assuredly nothing to reply; and thus at last I am constrained to confess that there is no one of all my former opinions which is not open to doubt, and this not merely owing to want of thought on my part, or through levity, but from cogent and maturely considered reasons. Henceforth, therefore, should I desire to discover something certain, I ought to refrain from assenting to these opinions no less scrupulously than in respect of what is manifestly false.

But it is not sufficient to have taken note of these conclusions; we must also be careful to keep them in mind. For long-established customary opinions perpetually recur in thought, long and familiar usage having given them the right to occupy my mind, even almost against my will, and to be masters of my belief. Nor shall I ever lose this habit of assenting to and of confiding in them, not at least so long as I consider them as in truth they are, namely, as opinions which, though in some fashion doubtful (as I have just shown), are still, none the less, highly probable and such as it is much more reasonable to believe than to deny. This is why I shall, as I think, be acting prudently if, taking a directly contrary line, I of set purpose employ every available device for the deceiving of myself, feigning that all these opinions are entirely false and imaginary. Then, in due course, having so balanced my old-time prejudices by this new prejudice that I cease to incline to one side more than to another, my judgment, no longer dominated by misleading usages, will not be hindered by them in the apprehension of things. In this course there can, I am convinced, be neither danger nor error. What I have under consideration is a question solely of knowledge, not of action, so that I cannot for the present be at fault as being over-ready to adopt a questioning attitude.

Accordingly I shall now suppose, not that a true God, who as such must be supremely good and the fountain of truth, but that some malignant genius exceedingly powerful and cunning has devoted all his powers in the deceiving of me; I shall suppose that the sky, the earth, colors, shapes, sounds and all external things are illusions and impostures of which this evil genius has availed himself for the abuse of my credulity; I shall consider myself as having no hands, no eyes, no flesh, no blood, nor any senses, but as falsely opining myself to possess all these things. Further, I shall obstinately persist in this way of thinking; and even if, while so doing, it may not be within my power to arrive at the knowledge of any truth, there is one thing I have it in me to do, viz., to suspend judgment, refusing assent to what is false. Thereby, thanks to this resolved firmness of mind, I shall be effectively guarding myself against being imposed upon by this deceiver, no matter how powerful or how craftily deceptive he may be.

This undertaking is, however, irksome and laborious, and a certain indolence drags me back into the course of my customary life. Just as a captive who has been enjoying in sleep an imaginary liberty, should he begin to suspect that his liberty is a dream, dreads awakening, and conspires with the agreeable illusions for the prolonging of the deception, so in similar fashion I gladly lapse back into my accustomed opinions. I dread to be wakened, in fear lest the wakefulness may have to be laboriously spent, not in the tranquilizing light of truth, but in the extreme darkness of the above-suggested questionings.

Chapter 4

Scientific
Revolutions

Chapter Preface

Before the Renaissance, education was strictly controlled by the church. Teachings about history, science, and the arts had to conform to biblical statements, as interpreted by the church. A scientist making claims that contradicted religious teachings could find himself in prison. However, the Renaissance, with its emphasis on reason, logic, and scientific observation, ushered in a new way of appreciating as well as acquiring knowledge. Reason and objective scientific observation were now promoted by the best minds of the age. This resulted in a steady stream of scientific discoveries and inventions that rattled traditional beliefs and changed the way people looked at themselves, their world, and their place in the universe.

The most significant scientific challenge to medieval thinking was the discovery that the earth was not the center of the universe, around which all the planets and the sun revolved. In advancing his theory, Polish astronomer Nicolaus Copernicus (1473–1543) shocked the world and alarmed the church, which maintained that the earth, because it was the most important place to God, was the center. Copernicus's theory threatened humanity's importance in the scheme of things. Even so, the church felt secure enough to sponsor his treatise, *The Revolutions of Celestial Spheres,* which was published the year he died. However, seventy years later, when Galileo Galilei (1564–1642), perfected the telescope in 1610, and was therefore able to confirm Copernicus's theories, the church was not so generous. Its authority already under attack from Catholic reformers, Protestants, and rebellious monarchs, the church reacted by trying Galileo for heresy. As punishment, he was forced to recant his theories and was placed under house arrest for the last eight years of his life.

But the genie was already out of the bottle and there was nothing the church could do to force it back in. Science crawled out from under the shadow of the church to become its own discipline with its own rules, and scientists were now dedicated to the search for truth, no matter what conventional, even sacred, beliefs might be proven wrong. Consequently, the Renaissance philosophy produced many inventions and scientific innovations that forever changed the world.

The Revolutions of the Celestial Spheres

Nicolaus Copernicus

When Polish astronomer Nicolaus Copernicus (1473–1543)
offered mathematical proof that the Earth rotated on an axis
and revolved around a stationary sun, he radically changed
the way people saw the world and their place in it. Conventional wisdom of the time, based mostly on second-century
Greek astronomer Ptolemy's incorrect theories and on traditional interpretation of biblical passages, taught that the Earth
was the center of the universe and the sun and planets
revolved around it. Copernican theory shattered not only the
science of that belief, but contributed to the Renaissance's
rethinking of humanity's position in the grand scheme of
creation. If people were not the center of the universe, perhaps they were not the most important beings in it.

In 1533, Copernicus's theories were presented to Pope
Clement VII (1478–1534), who quickly approved them and
requested that they be published. However, fearful of the outraged reaction already given by Protestant leaders, including
Martin Luther (1483–1546), Copernicus withheld permission
until 1540. His book, *On the Revolutions of the Celestial
Spheres*, excerpted below, was not published until 1543,
thirty years after he had first proposed his theories. Report-
edly, a finished copy of the book was brought to him on his
deathbed.

Excerpted from *Copernicus: On the Revolutions of the Celestial Spheres*, by Nicolaus Copernicus, translated by A.M. Duncan (London: David & Charles, 1976). Copyright © 1976 by
A.M. Duncan, New English translation. Reprinted by permission of the publisher.

*W*hy the ancients thought the Earth was at rest in the
middle of the universe as if it was the centre

Consequently it was by other arguments that the ancient
philosophers tried to assign the Earth to a position fixed at
the middle of the universe. The most powerful argument they
produce is that from heaviness and lightness. According to
them, the heaviest element is Earth, and all things which
have weight are carried towards it, striving towards the very
middle of it. For the Earth being globular, heavy bodies from
all directions are carried to it by their own nature at right angles to its surface, and if they were not stopped at the actual
surface would plunge towards its centre, seeing that the
straight line which meets a tangential plane where it touches
a sphere, at right angles, leads to the centre. But that which
is carried to the middle must, it seems to follow, rest at the
middle. All the more, therefore, will the whole Earth be at
rest in the middle, and that which receives all things which
fall into itself will remain immobile by its own weight. In
the same way they also try to prove the point by an argument
from motion, and by the nature of the thing itself. According to them [fourth-century Greek philosopher] Aristotle
says that the motion of a simple body is simple. Further, of
simple motions, one kind is up, another down. Wherefore
every simple motion is either towards the middle, which is
down; or away from the middle, which is up; or about the
middle and is itself circular. It is normal for earth and water,
which are regarded as heavy, to be carried down, that is to
seek the middle, but for air and fire, on the other hand, which
are endowed with lightness, to move upwards and away
from the middle. That is Aristotle's theory. If therefore, said
Ptolemy of Alexandria, the Earth were to revolve, at least
with a daily revolution, it would have to happen contrary to
what has just been said. For it would have to be an extremely
rapid motion, and its speed would be unsurpassable, to carry
the Earth round a complete circuit in twenty-four hours. Indeed things which are suddenly whirled round seem extremely unlikely to assemble together, and more likely to be
dispersed if they are united, unless they cohere and are held

together by solidity; and long since, said he, the Earth would have been scattered to the heavens (which is quite ridiculous) and destroyed, and all the less would living things and any other loose burdens have remained undisturbed. Nor would falling bodies go down in straight lines to the place ordained for them, and at right angles, for its swiftness would have moved it away while they fell. Also we should see clouds and everything else which was suspended in the air continually being carried westwards.

Refutation of the arguments quoted, and their insufficiency

From these and similar arguments, then, they say that the Earth is at rest in the middle of the universe, and that such is undoubtedly the state of affairs. Yet if anyone should hold the opinion that the Earth revolves, he will surely assert that its motion is natural, not violent. What is natural produces contrary effects to what is violent. For objects to which force or impulse is applied must necessarily be destroyed and cannot long subsist; but objects which exist naturally are in their proper state, and continue in their perfect form. There is therefore no need for Ptolemy to fear the scattering of the Earth and of all terrestrial objects in a revolution brought about by the workings of nature, which is far different from artifice, or what can be achieved by human abilities. Further, why is not the same question raised even more strongly about the universe, the motion of which must be swifter in proportion as the heaven is greater than the Earth? Or has the heaven become so immense, because it is drawn outwards from the middle by a motion of ineffable strength, that it would collapse if it were not at rest? Certainly if this reasoning were to be accepted, the magnitude of the heaven will rise to infinity. For in proportion as it is thrown higher by the impulse of the motion, so the motion will be swifter, on account of the continual increase in the circumference which it must traverse in the space of twenty-four hours; and on the other hand as the motion increased, so would the immensity of the heaven. So the velocity would increase the magnitude, and the magnitude the velocity, to infinity. But according to that axiom in physics, that what is infinite cannot be traversed, nor moved by any means, the heaven will necessarily be at rest. But they say that outside the heaven there is no body, no place, no empty space, in fact nothing whatsoever, and therefore there is nothing to which the heaven can go out. In that case it is remarkable indeed if something can be restrained by nothing. But if the heaven be infinite, and finite only in its hollow interior, perhaps it will be more clearly proved that there is nothing outside the heaven, since every single thing will be within it, whatever amount of space it occupies, but the heaven will remain immovable. For the strongest argument by which they try to establish that the universe is finite, is its motion. Therefore let us leave the question whether the universe is finite or infinite for the natural philosophers to argue. What we do know for certain is that the Earth is limited by its poles and bounded by a globular surface. Why therefore do we still hesitate to concede movement to that which has a shape naturally fitted for it, rather than believe that the whole universe is shifting, al-

Nicolaus Copernicus

though its limit is unknown and cannot be known? And why should we not admit that the daily revolution itself is apparent in the heaven, but real in the Earth; and the case is just as if [first-century B.C. Roman poet Publius Vergilius Maro] Virgil's [fictional narrator of epic poem, *Aeneid*] Aeneas were saying 'We sail out from the harbour, and the land and cities recede'? For when a ship is floating along in calm weather, everything which is outside her is perceived by those who are sailing as moving by a reflection of that motion, and on the other hand they think that they are at rest along with everything that is with them. Naturally the same can happen in the motion of the Earth, so that the whole universe is thought to go round. Then what should we say about clouds, and other things of all kinds which are suspended in the air, or sinking and rising upwards again? Only that it is not just the Earth with the element of water which is joined to it which moves in this way, but also a considerable part of the air, and anything else which has a similar affinity with the Earth, whether the neighbouring air takes on the same nature as Earth through being mixed with earthy and watery material, or whether the motion of the air is acquired, because it shares it with the Earth by its perpetual revolution and the absence of resistance through contiguity. On the other hand it is with equal surprise that they speak of the upper region of the air following the motion of the heaven, which is indicated by those suddenly appearing stars, I mean those called comets or Pogoniae (Bearded Ones) by the Greeks, the production of which is allocated to that region, and which rise and set like the other stars. We can say that this upper part of the air does not partake of the Earth's motion on account of its great distance from the Earth. Similarly the air which is nearest to the Earth will appear still, and objects suspended in it will be set in motion only by wind or some other impulse this way or that. For what is the difference between a wind in the air and a wave on the sea? We have indeed to admit that the motion of falling and rising bodies is a dual motion in comparison with the universe, and is no less a compound of straight and circular motion. For the parts which are brought down by their own weight, since they are chiefly earthy, undoubtedly keep the same nature as the whole. The same applies to things which are thrown upwards by the force of their fiery nature. For not only is a fire here on Earth fed chiefly by earthy material, but they define flame as nothing more than burning smoke. However it is a property of fire to expand whatever it enters, which it does with such force that it cannot be restrained by any means or by any mechanisms from fulfilling its purpose by bursting its bonds. But its expansive motion is away from the middle towards the circumference; and similarly if something from Earthly parts has caught fire, it is carried upwards away from the middle. It follows that their assertion that the motion of a simple body is simple is justified in the first instance for circular motion, so long as the body retains its own natural place and its own unity. In its place indeed no motion other than circular is possible, if it remains wholly within its own volume as if at rest. Straight line motion is imparted to objects which wander or are pushed from their own natural place, or in any way overstep this volume. But nothing is more repugnant to the whole pattern and form of the universe than for something to be out of its own place. Hence straight line motion does not occur except in objects not in their proper state, when they are separated from the whole of which they are part, and detract from its unity. Furthermore things which move up and down, even without circular motion, are not performing a uniform and even simple motion. For on account of their lightness or the impulse of their own weight they cannot be slowed down; and any objects which drop start by performing a slow motion and increase their speed as they fall. On the other hand we perceive that this Earthly fire (for we see no other) when it rushes upwards at once grows faint, as if acknowledging the cause of the violence to be the terrestrial material. Yet circular motion always goes round evenly, for its cause is unfailing; but objects moving in a straight line lose the cause which accelerates them, and having achieved their own place by it they cease to be light or heavy, and that motion ceases. Since therefore circular motion belongs to wholes, and straight line motion to parts, we can say that circular motion accompanies straight just as an animal can at the same time be in the class of sick things. Surely Aristotle's division of simple motion into three types, away from the middle, towards the middle, and round the middle, will be regarded merely as an intellectual division; just as we distinguish between a line, a point and a surface, although one cannot exist without the other, and none of them without a body. A further point is that immobility is considered a more noble and divine state than that of change and instability, which is for that reason more appropriate to the Earth than to the universe. I also add that it would seem rather absurd to ascribe motion to that which contains and locates, and not rather to that which is contained and located, that is the Earth. Lastly, since it is evident that the wandering stars are sometimes nearer, sometimes further from the Earth, this also will be an example of motion of a single body which is both round the middle, by which they mean the centre, away from the middle, and towards it. Motion round the midpoint must therefore be accepted more generally, and as satisfactory, provided that each motion is motion about its own midpoint. You see then that from all these arguments the mobility of the Earth is more probable than its immobility, especially in the daily revolution, as that is particularly fitting for the Earth.

Concerning the Use of Biblical Quotations in Matters of Science

Galileo Galilei

> Although Nicolaus Copernicus (1473–1543) laid the ground-
> work for the modern scientific study of the heavens, it was
> Italian astronomer, mathematician, and physicist Galileo
> Galilei (1564–1642) who both built on those theories and
> bore the hardships because of how deeply they challenged
> conventional beliefs. Galileo's accomplishments characterize
> the great leaps in science that the Renaissance encouraged.
> He invented the thermometer, wrote about the principles later
> expanded by Sir Isaac Newton's first two laws of motion, and
> experimented with gravitation. Because of works like this, he
> is considered the founder of modern mechanics and experi-
> mental physics, as well as the founder of the modern experi-
> mental method later expanded on by French Renaissance
> philosopher and mathematician René Descartes (1596–1650).
>
> In 1610, Galileo perfected the telescope, which allowed
> him to see mountains on the moon as well as discover new
> planets. It also allowed him to amass overwhelming evidence
> that confirmed Copernicus's theory that the Earth revolved
> around the Sun, which he presented in his book *The Sidereal
> Messenger*. Although the Catholic Church had been support-
> ive of Copernicus, Galileo found church authorities less
> receptive. In 1632, he was tried for heresy in Rome and

Excerpted from *Discoveries and Opinions of Galileo*, by Galileo Galilei, translated by
Stillman Drake (New York: Doubleday Anchor Books, 1957). Copyright © 1957 by Stillman Drake. Reprinted with permission.

forced to recant his theories regarding the Earth's position in the solar system. He spent the last eight years of his life under house arrest.

The following passage from his "Letter to Grand Duchess of Tuscany Concerning Use of Biblical Quotations in Matters of Science" in 1615 reveals, not a man using science to overthrow the church's position, but rather a religious man using science to defend the church. He feared that the church's support of inaccurate scientific theories would eventually weaken its position among adherents. The Grand Duchess addressed in the letter was part of an influential Italian family. Her brother was a cardinal who unsuccessfully defended Galileo's theories to the pope. In the letter, he reminds the Duchess of the church's long-standing practice of interpreting Scriptures allegorically whenever there was a conflict between biblical passages and proven scientific facts.

Some years ago, as Your Serene Highness well knows, I discovered in the heavens many things that had not been seen before our own age. The novelty of these things, as well as some consequences which followed from them in contradiction to the physical notions commonly held among academic philosophers, stirred up against me no small number of professors—as if I had placed these things in the sky with my own hands in order to upset nature and overturn the sciences. They seemed to forget that the increase of known truths stimulates the investigation, establishment, and growth of the arts; not their diminution or destruction.

Showing a greater fondness for their own opinions than for truth, they sought to deny and disprove the new things which, if they had cared to look for themselves, their own senses would have demonstrated to them. To this end they hurled various charges and published numerous writings filled with vain arguments, and they made the grave mistake of sprinkling these with passages taken from places in the Bible which they had failed to understand properly, and which were ill suited to their purposes.

These men would perhaps not have fallen into such error

had they but paid attention to a most useful doctrine of [fifth-century Catholic theologian] St. Augustine's, relative to our making positive statements about things which are obscure and hard to understand by means of reason alone. Speaking of a certain physical conclusion about the heavenly bodies, he wrote: "Now keeping always our respect for moderation in grave piety, we ought not to believe anything inadvisedly on a dubious point, lest in favor to our error we conceive a prejudice against something that truth hereafter may reveal to be not contrary in any way to the sacred books of either the Old or the New Testament."

No Denying the Truth

Well, the passage of time has revealed to everyone the truths that I previously set forth; and, together with the truth of the facts, there has come to light the great difference in attitude between those who simply and dispassionately refused to admit the discoveries to be true, and those who combined with their incredulity some reckless passion of their own. Men who were well grounded in astronomical and physical science were persuaded as soon as they received my first message. There were others who denied them or remained in doubt only because of their novel and unexpected character, and because they had not yet had the opportunity to see for themselves. These men have by degrees come to be satisfied. But some, besides allegiance to their original error, possess I know not what fanciful interest in remaining hostile not so much toward the things in question as toward their discoverer. No longer being able to deny them, these men now take refuge in obstinate silence, but being more than ever exasperated by that which has pacified and quieted other men, they divert their thoughts to other fancies and seek new ways to damage me.

I should pay no more attention to them than to those who previously contradicted me—at whom I always laugh, being assured of the eventual outcome—were it not that in their new calumnies [slanders] and persecutions I perceive that they do not stop at proving themselves more learned than I am (a claim which I scarcely contest), but go so far as to cast against me imputations of crimes which must be, and are, more abhorrent to me than death itself. I cannot remain satisfied merely to know that the injustice of this is recognized by those who are acquainted with these men and with me, as perhaps it is not known to others.

Damning Accusations

Persisting in their original resolve to destroy me and everything mine by any means they can think of, these men are aware of my views in astronomy and philosophy. They know that as to the arrangement of the parts of the universe, I hold the sun to be situated motionless in the center of the revolution of the celestial orbs while the earth rotates on its axis and revolves about the sun. They know also that I support this position not only by refuting the arguments of [second-century Greek astronomer] Ptolemy and [fourth-century B.C. Greek philosopher] Aristotle, but by producing many counter-arguments; in particular, some which relate to physical effects whose causes can perhaps be assigned in no other way. In addition there are astronomical arguments derived from many things in my new celestial discoveries that plainly confute the Ptolemaic system while admirably agreeing with and confirming the contrary hypothesis. Possibly because they are disturbed by the known truth of other propositions of mine which differ from those commonly held, and therefore mistrusting their defense so long as they confine themselves to the field of philosophy, these men have resolved to fabricate a shield for their fallacies out of the mantle of pretended religion and the authority of the Bible. These they apply, with little judgment, to the refutation of arguments that they do not understand and have not even listened to.

First they have endeavored to spread the opinion that such propositions in general are contrary to the Bible and are consequently damnable and heretical. They know that it is human nature to take up causes whereby a man may oppress his neighbor, no matter how unjustly, rather than those from which a man may receive some just encouragement. Hence they have had no trouble in finding men who would preach the damnability and heresy of the new doctrine from their very pulpits with unwonted confidence, thus doing impious and inconsiderate injury not only to that doctrine and its followers but to all mathematics and mathematicians in general. Next, becoming bolder, and hoping (though vainly) that this seed which first took root in their hypocritical minds would send out branches and ascend to heaven, they began scattering rumors among the people that before long this doctrine would be condemned by the supreme authority. They know, too, that official condemnation would not only suppress the two propositions which I have mentioned, but would render damnable all other astronomical and physical statements and observations that have any necessary relation or connection with these.

In order to facilitate their designs, they seek so far as possible (at least among the common people) to make this opinion seem new and to belong to me alone. They pretend not to know that its author, or rather its restorer and confirmer, was [sixteenth-century Polish astronomer] Nicholas Copernicus; and that he was not only a Catholic, but a priest and a canon [member of certain Roman Catholic orders]. He was in fact so esteemed by the church that when the Lateran Council under [sixteenth-century pope] Leo X took up the correction of the church calendar, Copernicus was called to Rome from the most remote parts of Germany to undertake its reform. . . .

Correctly Interpreting Scripture

Now as to the false aspersions which they so unjustly seek to cast upon me, I have thought it necessary to justify myself in the eyes of all men, whose judgment in matters of religion and of reputation I must hold in great esteem. I shall therefore discourse of the particulars which these men produce to make this opinion detested and to have it condemned not merely as false but as heretical. To this end they make a shield of their hypocritical zeal for religion. They go about invoking the Bible, which they would have minister to their deceitful purposes. Contrary to the sense of the Bible and the intention of the holy Fathers, if I am not mistaken, they would extend such authorities until even in purely physical matters—where faith is not involved—they would have us altogether abandon reason and the evidence of our senses in favor of some biblical passage, though under the surface meaning of its words this passage may contain a different sense.

I hope to show that I proceed with much greater piety than they do, when I argue not against condemning this book, but

Galileo Galilei

against condemning it in the way they suggest—that is, without understanding it, weighing it, or so much as reading it. For Copernicus never discusses matters of religion or faith, nor does he use arguments that depend in any way upon the authority of sacred writings which he might have interpreted erroneously. He stands always upon physical conclusions pertaining to the celestial motions, and deals with them by astronomical and geometrical demonstrations, founded primarily upon sense experiences and very exact observations. He did not ignore the Bible, but he knew very well that if his doctrine were proved, then it could not contradict the Scriptures when they were rightly understood. . . .

The reason produced for condemning the opinion that the earth moves and the sun stands still is that in many places in the Bible one may read that the sun moves and the earth stands still. Since the Bible cannot err, it follows as a necessary consequence that anyone takes an erroneous and heretical position who maintains that the sun is inherently motionless and the earth movable.

With regard to this argument, I think in the first place that it is very pious to say and prudent to affirm that the holy Bible can never speak untruth—whenever its true meaning is understood. But I believe nobody will deny that it is often very abstruse, and may say things which are quite different from what its bare words signify. Hence in expounding the Bible if one were always to confine oneself to the unadorned grammatical meaning, one might fall into error. Not only contradictions and propositions far from true might thus be made to appear in the Bible, but even grave heresies and follies. Thus it would be necessary to assign to God feet, hands, and eyes, as well as corporeal and human affections, such as anger, repentance, hatred, and sometimes even the forgetting of things past and ignorance of those to come. These propositions uttered by the Holy Ghost were set down in that manner by the sacred scribes in order to accommodate them to the capacities of the common people, who are rude and unlearned. For the sake of those who deserve to be separated from the herd, it is necessary that wise expositors should produce the true senses of such passages, together with the special reasons for which they were set down in these words. This doctrine is so widespread and so definite with all theologians that it would be superfluous to adduce evidence for it.

Hence I think that I may reasonably conclude that whenever the Bible has occasion to speak of any physical conclusion (especially those which are very abstruse and hard to understand), the rule has been observed of avoiding confusion in the minds of the common people which would render them contumacious toward the higher mysteries. Now the Bible, merely to condescend to popular capacity, has not hesitated to obscure some very important pronouncements, attributing to God himself some qualities extremely remote from (and even contrary to) His essence. Who, then, would positively declare that this principle has been set aside, and the Bible has confined itself rigorously to the bare and restricted sense of its words, when speaking but casually of the earth, of water, of the sun, or of any other created thing? Especially in view of the fact that these things in no way concern the primary purpose of the sacred writings, which is the service of God and the salvation of souls—matters infinitely beyond the comprehension of the common people.

Begin from Sense-Experience

This being granted, I think that in discussions of physical problems we ought to begin not from the authority of scriptural passages, but from sense-experiences and necessary demonstrations; for the holy Bible and the phenomena of nature proceed alike from the divine Word, the former as the dictate of the Holy Ghost and the latter as the observant executrix of God's commands. It is necessary for the Bible, in order to be accommodated to the understanding of every man, to speak many things which appear to differ from the absolute truth so far as the bare meaning of the words is concerned. But Nature, on the other hand, is inexorable and immutable; she never transgresses the laws imposed upon her, or cares a whit whether her abstruse reasons and methods of operation are understandable to men. For that reason it appears that nothing physical which sense-experience sets before our eyes, or which necessary demonstrations prove to us, ought to be called in question (much less condemned) upon the testimony of biblical passages which may have some different meaning beneath their words. For the Bible is not chained in every expression to conditions as strict as those which govern all physical effects; nor is God any less excellently revealed in Nature's actions than in the sacred statements of the Bible. Perhaps this is what Tertullian meant by these words:

"We conclude that God is known first through Nature, and then again, more particularly, by doctrine; by Nature in His works, and by doctrine in His revealed word."

From this I do not mean to infer that we need not have an extraordinary esteem for the passages of holy Scripture. On the contrary, having arrived at any certainties in physics, we ought to utilize these as the most appropriate aids in the true exposition of the Bible and in the investigation of those meanings which are necessarily contained therein, for these must be concordant with demonstrated truths. I should judge that the authority of the Bible was designed to persuade men of those articles and propositions which, surpassing all human reasoning, could not be made credible by science, or by any other means than through the very mouth of the Holy Spirit.

Scientific Correspondences

Johannes Kepler

Before the Renaissance, astronomy (the observation of heavenly objects) and astrology (using those observations to predict events and human behavior) were closely aligned. Rulers and average citizens alike consulted astrologers for advice. German Johannes Kepler (1571–1630), who served as imperial mathematician to Holy Roman Emperor Rudolph II (1552–1612), was renowned as both astronomer and astrologer. A highly accomplished scientist, he discovered the three principles of planetary motion, further explained the spatial organization of the solar system, and founded modern optics when he presented the first accurate description of how human beings see. Physicist Albert Einstein described Kepler as a true Renaissance scientist in that he sought truth despite the personal cost to him: "Neither by poverty, nor incomprehension of the contemporaries who ruled over the conditions of his life and work, did he allow himself to be crippled or discouraged. In addition, he dealt with a field of knowledge that immediately endangered the adherent of religious truth."

In the following letters, Kepler discusses his theories, including that there is life on stars, with contemporaries such as astronomer Galileo Galilei (1564–1642). In them we can see Kepler struggling with the impact of Galileo's discoveries on astrology as well as the impact on science of the Catholic Church's execution of some thinkers for heresy.

Excerpted from *Johannes Kepler: Life and Letters*, by Johannes Kepler, edited by Carola Baumgardt (New York: Philosophical Library, 1951). Copyright © 1951 by Philosophical Library Publishers. Reprinted with permission.

*T*o *Italian astronomer Galileo Galilei*
                                    Graz, October 13th, 1597

I received your letter of August 4th on September 1st. It was a double pleasure to me. First, because I became friends with you, the Italian, and second because of the agreement in which we find ourselves concerning Copernican cosmography.[1] As you invite me kindly at the end of your letter to enter into correspondence with you, and I myself feel greatly tempted to do so, I will not let pass the occasion of sending you a letter with the present young nobleman. For I am sure, if your time has allowed it, you have meanwhile obtained a closer knowledge of my book. And so a great desire has taken hold of me, to learn your judgment. For this is my way, to urge all those to whom I have written to express their candid opinion. Believe me, the sharpest criticism of one single understanding man means much more to me than the thoughtless applause of the great masses.

I would, however, have wished that you who have such a keen insight [into everything] would choose another way [to reach your practical aims]. By the strength of your personal example you advise us, in a cleverly veiled manner, to go out of the way of general ignorance and [warn us against exposing ourselves to] the furious attacks of the scholarly crowd. (In this you are following the lead of [fifth-century B.C. Greek philosopher] Plato and [sixth-century B.C. Greek mathematician] Pythagoras, our true masters.) But after the beginning of a tremendous enterprise has been made in our time, and furthered by so many learned mathematicians, and after the statement that the earth moves can no longer be regarded as something new, would it not be better to pull the rolling wagon to its destination with united effort. . . . For it is not only you Italians who do not believe that they move unless they feel it, but we in Germany, too, in no way make ourselves popular with this idea. Yet there are ways in which we protect ourselves against these difficulties. . . . Be of

---

1. Sixteenth-century Polish astronomer Nicolaus Copernicus first theorized that the sun was fixed and the planets orbited it.

good cheer, Galileo, and appear in public. If I am not mistaken there are only a few among the distinguished mathematicians of Europe who would dissociate themselves from us. So great is the power of truth. If Italy seems less suitable for your publication and if you have to expect difficulties there, perhaps Germany will offer us more freedom. But enough of this. Please let me know, at least privately if you do not want to do so publicly, what you have discovered in favor of Copernicus.

Now I want to ask you for an observation; as I possess no instruments I must turn to other people. Do you possess a quadrant which shows minutes and quarterminutes? If so, then, please, observe at about the time of the 19th of December the smallest and the largest altitude of the middle star of the tail in the great dipper. Likewise observe about December 26th both heights of the polar star. Also observe the first star about the 19th of March 1598 in its height at midnight, the second about September 28th, also around midnight. If, as I wish, there could be shown a difference between the two observations of one or another minute or even 10' to 15', this would be proof of something of great importance for all astronomy. If there is no difference shown, however, we shall earn all the same together the fame of having become aware of an important problem hitherto not noticed by anybody. [Fixed-star parallax]. . . . Farewell and answer me with a very long letter.

To German mathematician Johann Georg Herwart von Hohenburg

Graz, March 26th, 1598

. . . You think from the winds and the movements of the oceans one could deduce reasons for the movement of the earth. I too have some ideas concerning these things. Galileo, a mathematician of Padua, assured me that he could quite correctly derive from the Copernican hypothesis the origin of very many natural phenomena which could not be explained by common hypotheses of others, though he did not mention details. On this occasion I also thought of the tides. Reflecting on these phenomena, it seems to me that we must not exclude the moon so far as we can deduce from it the calculation of the tides, and I think we can do that. He who ascribes the movement of the oceans to the movement of the earth refers to a forced movement; but he who lets the oceans follow the moon, in a certain way makes this movement a natural one. . . . In short, the hypotheses are not new but the ways of using them are new; they are a mixture of the old hypotheses with the new ones of Copernicus. I think thus: as we astronomers are priests of the highest God in regard to the book of nature, we are bound to think of the praise of God and not of the glory of our own capacities. Who is convinced of that does not publish light-mindedly what he does not believe himself. . . . I am content with the honor of having my discovery guard the doors of the sanctuary in which Copernicus performs the service at the higher altar. . . .

To Johann Georg Herwart von Hohenburg

Prague, March 28, 1605

. . . You ask me, Magnificence, about the hypotheses of Copernicus and you seem to be pleased that I insist on my opinion. . . .

[One of my main ideas aimed against [sixteenth-century Danish astronomer] Tycho [Brahe] is] if the sun moves round the earth, then it must, of necessity, along with the other planets become sometimes faster, sometimes slower in its movements, and this without following fixed courses, since there are none. But this is incredible. Furthermore, the sun which is so much higher ranking than the unimportant earth would have to be moved by the earth in the same way as the five other planets are put in motion by the sun. That is completely absurd. Therefore it is much more plausible that the earth together with the five planets is put in motion by the sun and only the moon by the earth.

To German physician Johann Georg Brengger

Heidelberg, November 30, 1607

. . . You think the nature of the starglobes quite pure and simple. I should think that they are similar to our earth. Being a philosopher you quote from a philosopher. If one would ask him he would refer to experience. But experience is silent, as no one ever visited the stars. Experience, therefore, says neither yes nor no. I refer in my probable inference to the similarity of the moon to the earth. On the moon much is similar to the terrestrial conditions. In my opinion there is also humidity on the stars . . . and therefore living creatures who benefit from these conditions. Not only the unfortunate Bruno who was burned in Rome on red-hot coals, but also the venerated Brahe was of the opinion that there are living creatures on the stars. I, too, am a follower of this opinion especially as I maintain with Aristarchus, that the earth has motion in common with the planets. . . .

To Johann Georg Brengger

Prague, April 5, 1608
. . . I heard . . . that Bruno has been burnt in Rome; he is said to have been unyielding during the execution. He maintained the futility of all forms of religion and transformed the divine being into the world, into circles and points. . . .

My opinion that there are unseen comets in the sky is disputed by many. One asks how I could know this. But I do not say that I do know it, I only think it probable. You believe that one should see them, if they exist. I deny this. For, if they follow their course far away from the earth, it is quite possible, if they are small, that one does not see them. What does Aristotle say? Does he not say that many pass in the daytime which one cannot see because of daylight? Who told this to Aristotle? I did not say and also do not believe that the matter of the comets has been created out of nothing. To create means to create from matter even if this already existed. It is not absurd either to assume that the starglobes evaporate into the ether. How, if the earth also evaporates into the ether? Whither, do you think, escapes the matter which is left after the burning of meteors? Do you not daily see how large pieces of wood burn? Weigh the ashes accurately and conclude therefrom how much matter escapes upwards. . . .

You prophesied rightly that the theologians would be offended. They have prohibited indeed the printing of the book in Leipzig, because of the last sentence about the creation of the spirit. I have therefore changed the straightforward expression in the Latin text. Yet I do not believe that my opinion is so absurd. . . . I believe that the spirit is not created out of nothing, but of heavenly matter, and afterwards it is illuminated and instructed by a ray out of God's image. . . .

To Galileo Galilei

Prague, August 9, 1610

I have received your observations on the Medicean stars from the Ambassador of his Highness the Grand Duke of Tuscany. You have aroused in me a passionate desire to see your instruments, so that I at last, like you, might enjoy the great performance in the sky. Of the oculars which we have here the best has a tenfold enlargement, the others hardly a threefold; the only one which I have gives a twentyfold enlargement, but the light is very weak. The reason for this is not unknown to me and I see how the intensity could be improved, but one hesitates to spend the money.

. . . In my opinion, no one is entitled to charge a person with having taken over another's ideas unless he is able to recognize and . . . understand the new, rare, and beautifully original ideas which the other has pronounced. To me it is an insult . . . if someone wants to praise me because of my reputation in order to slander others. Nothing annoys me more than the praise of such a man; what an outcast of a human being! He fantastically ascribes to me doubts about the value of your discoveries, because I allow everyone his own opinion. What lack of judgment! The considerations of others need not necessarily be in accord with my own. Regarding something as true, I am, nevertheless, able to tolerate others who are not of the same opinion.

. . . O, you wise Pythagoras, who believed that the majesty of philosophy is present in nothing but silence! But now the die is cast. You, my Galileo, have opened the holy of the holiest of the skies. What else can you do but despise the noise which has been created. . . . The crowd takes vengeance on itself by remaining in eternal ignorance in consequence of its contempt for philosophy.

The Cause of Humanity's Miseries

Robert Burton

English scholar, writer, and Anglican clergyman Robert Burton (1577–1640) epitomized the Renaissance scientific approach with the publication of his massive work, *The Anatomy of Melancholy* (1621). Melancholy, or melancholia, is characterized by deep depression and hopelessness. As a clergyman, Burton confronted people in this condition on a daily basis, for which he applied spiritual remedies. Burton himself admitted he suffered from melancholy, saying that he wrote about melancholy to cure himself of it. However, not content to rely on spiritual explanations and cures, he set about to study depression on a physical, psychological, and cultural basis. To his critics who suggested he should stick to healing the soul, he argued that the spiritual and medicine were closely allied and needed to work together to cure the whole person.

The following selection from *The Anatomy of Melancholy* demonstrates the extent of Burton's scholarly knowledge in the number of references he makes to other writers and works. But it also reveals his strong conviction that love of God is the ultimate source of mental health.

M an, the most excellent and noble creature of the World, *the principal and mighty work of God, wonder of Nature,* as [sixth-century B.C. Persian religious leader] Zoroaster calls him; *the marvel of marvels,* as [fifth-century

Excerpted from "The First Partition," by Robert Burton, *The Anatomy of Melancholy*, edited by Floyd Dell and Paul Jordan-Smith (New York: Tudor Publishing Company, 1927).

B.C. Greek philosopher] Plato; *the Abridgement and Epitome of the World,* as [first-century Roman scientist Gaius Plinius Secundus] Pliny; a Microcosm, a little world, Sovereign Lord of the Earth, Viceroy of the World, sole Commander and Governor of all the Creatures in it: to whose Empire they are subject in particular, and yield obedience; far surpassing all the rest, not in body only, but in soul; created in God's own *Image,* to that immortal and incorporeal substance, with all the faculties and powers belonging unto it; was at first pure, divine, perfect, happy, created after God in true holiness and righteousness; Like God, free from all manner of infirmities, and put in Paradise, to know God, to praise and glorify him, to do his will: So that God might bring forth the Godlike, (as an old Poet saith) to propagate the Church.

The Fall of Man

But this most noble creature, (one exclaims) O pitiful change! is fallen from that he was, and forfeited his estate, become a wretched mannikin, a castaway, a caitiff [despicable person], one of the most miserable creatures of the world, if he be considered in his own nature, an unregenerate man, and so much obscured by his fall (that some few reliques excepted) he is inferior to a beast: *man in honour that understandeth not, is like unto beasts that perish,* so [tenth-century B.C. king of Israel and Judah] David esteems him: a monster by stupend metamorphosis, a fox, a dog, a hog, what not? How much altered from that he was; before blessed and happy, now miserable and accursed! . . .

The impulsive cause of these miseries in man, this privation [lack of comforts or necessities of life] or destruction of God's image, the cause of death and diseases, of all temporal [worldly as opposed to spiritual] and eternal punishments, was the sin of our first parent Adam, in eating of the forbidden fruit, by the devil's instigation and allurement. His disobedience, pride, ambition, intemperance, incredulity, curiosity; from whence proceeded original sin, and that general corruption of mankind, as from a fountain flowed all bad inclinations, and actual transgressions, which cause our several calamities inflicted upon us for our sins. And this belike is that which our fabulous Poets have shadowed unto us in the tale of Pandora's box, which, being opened through her curiosity, filled the world full of all manner of diseases. It is not curiosity alone, but those other crying sins of ours, which pull these several plagues and miseries upon our heads. For where there is sin, there is a storm, as [fifth-century Christian leader Saint John] Chrysostom well observes. *Fools by reason of their transgression, and because of their iniquities, are afflicted. Fear cometh like sudden desolation, and destruction like a whirlwind, affliction and anguish, because they did not fear God.* Are you shaken with wars? . . . is your health crushed with raging diseases? is mankind generally tormented with epidemical maladies? *'tis all for your sins. . . .*

Misery Is God's Punishment

To punish therefore this blindness and obstinacy of ours, as a concomitant cause, and principal agent, is God's just judgement, in bringing these calamities upon us, to chastise us, I say, for our sins, and to satisfy God's wrath. For the law requires obedience or punishment, as you may read at large: *If they will not obey the Lord, and keep his commandments and ordinances, then all these curses shall come upon them. Cursed in the town and in the field, &c. Cursed in the fruit of the body, &c. The Lord shall send thee trouble and shame, because of thy wickedness.* And a little after, *The Lord shall smite thee with the botch of Egypt, and with emrods, and scab, and itch, and thou canst not be healed. With madness, blindness, and astonishing of heart.* This [first-century Christian leader] Paul seconds, *Tribulation and anguish on the soul of every man that doth evil.* Or else these chastisements are inflicted upon us for our humiliation, to exercise and try our patience here in this life, to bring us home, to make us to know God and ourselves, to inform & teach us wisdom. . . . As Pliny well perceived, in sickness the mind reflects upon itself, with judgement surveys itself, and abhors its former courses; insomuch that he concludes to his friend [second-century Greek philosopher] Maximus, that it were the period of all philosophy, if we could so continue sound, or perform but a part of that which we promised to do, being sick. *Whoso is wise, then, will consider these things,* as David did, and whatsoever fortune befall him, make use of it. If he be in sorrow, need, sickness, or any other adversity, seriously to recount with himself, why this or that malady, misery, this or that incurable disease, is inflicted upon him; it may be for his good, truly it is well, as Peter said of his daughter's ague. Bodily sickness is for his soul's health, had he not been visited, he had utterly perished. . . .

The Devil's Influence

We can most part foresee these epidemical diseases, and likely avoid them. Dearths, tempests, plagues, our Astrologers foretell us; earthquakes, inundations, ruins of houses, consuming fires, come by little and little, or make some noise before-hand; but the knaveries, impostures, injuries, and villanies, of men no art can avoid. We can keep our professed enemies from our cities, by gates, walls, and towers, defend ourselves from thieves and robbers by watchfulness and weapons; but this malice of men, and their pernicious endeavours, no caution can divert, no vigilancy foresee, we have so many secret plots and devices to mischief one another.

Sometimes by the Devil's help, as Magicians, Witches: sometimes by impostures, mixtures, poisons, stratagems, single combats, wars, we hack and hew, as if we were, like Cadmus' soldiers [in Greek mythology, he built an army from dragon's teeth], born to consume one another. 'Tis an ordinary thing to read of a hundred and two hundred thousand men slain in a battle; besides all manner of tortures, brazen bulls, racks, wheels, strappadoes, guns, engines, &c. We have invented more torturing instruments than there be several members in a man's body, as [third-century Christian theologian Saint] Cyprian well observes. To come nearer yet, our own parents by their offences, indiscretion, and intemperance, are our mortal enemies. *The fathers have eaten sour grapes, and the children's teeth are set on edge.* They cause our grief many times, and put upon us hereditary diseases, inevitable infirmities: they torment us, & we are ready to injure our posterity;

Like to produce still more degenerate stock, (HORACE) and the latter end of the world, as Paul foretold, is still like to be worst. We are thus bad by nature, bad by kind, but far worse by art, every man the greatest enemy unto himself. We study many times to undo ourselves, abusing those good things which God hath bestowed upon us, health, wealth, strength, wit, learning, art, memory, to our own destruction; you owe to yourself your own ruin. As [second-century B.C. Jewish warrior] Judas Maccabaeus killed [second-century B.C. ruler who oppressed the Jews] Apollonius with his own weapons, we arm our selves to our own overthrows; and use reason, art, judgement, all that should help us, as so many instruments to undo us. [In Greek mythology, chief Trojan warrior] Hector gave [king and warrior who fought in Trojan War] Ajax a sword, which, so long as he fought against enemies, served for his help and defence; but after he began to hurt harmless creatures with it, turned to his own hurtless bowels. Those excellent means God hath bestowed on us, well employed, cannot but much avail us; but if otherwise perverted, they ruin and confound us: and so by reason of our indiscretion and weakness they commonly do, we have too many instances. This S. Austin [refers to fifth-century Christian theologian St. Augustine] acknowledgeth of himself in his humble Confessions, *promptness of wit, memory, eloquence, they were God's good gifts, but he did not use them to his glory.* If you will particularly know how, and by what means, consult Physicians, and they will tell you, that it is in offending in some of those six non-natural things, of which I shall after dilate more at large; they are the causes of our infirmities, our surfeiting, and drunkenness, our immoderate insatiable lust, and prodigious riot. It is a true saying, the board consumes more than the sword. Our intemperance it is that pulls so many several incurable diseases upon our heads, that hastens old age, perverts our temperature, and brings upon us sudden death. And last of all, that which crucifies us most, is our own folly, madness (Whom [head of the Roman gods] Jupiter would destroy, he first drives mad; by subtraction of his assisting grace God permits it), weakness, want of government, our facility and proneness in yielding to several lusts, in giving way to every passion and perturbation of the mind: by which means we metamorphose ourselves, and degenerate into beasts. . . . As long as we are ruled by reason, correct our inordinate appetite, and conform ourselves to God's word, are as so many living saints: but if we give reins to lust, anger, ambition, pride, and follow our own ways, we degenerate into beasts, transform ourselves, overthrow our constitutions, provoke God to anger, and heap upon us this of *Melancholy,* and all kinds of incurable diseases, as a just and deserved punishment of our sins.

Chapter 5

Humanist Expression in Art

Chapter Preface

The Renaissance brought about a flourishing of all the arts, from architecture to painting to poetry, though not without a struggle. Just as Renaissance scientists and philosophers were determined to find truth, no matter what traditional beliefs were upset, so artists were determined to go where their private thoughts and emotions led them, even if it shattered cherished conventional beliefs. While the art of the Middle Ages focused on praising God and disapproving of humans and their spiritual weakness, Renaissance art focused on celebrating humans, both in their strengths and weaknesses. The art of the Middle Ages portrayed life as a grim punishment to be endured for the sake of a better afterlife. The art of the Renaissance portrayed life as a sensuous experience with a balance of both hardships and pleasures.

This new sensuality in painting was expressed both by exploring new techniques and by broadening the subject matter. The most important change in technique was the use of perspective. Medieval paintings deliberately presented flat, two-dimensional figures. Renaissance artists, however, developed three-dimensional perspective, making subjects appear more natural. This paved the way for other innovations, such as the use of vivid colors and the portrayal of subjects with more expressive faces and more physical movement. Though religious subject matter was still popular, artists felt free to paint other, more secular subjects. Portraits of nudes became fashionable as artists celebrated the human body in all its glory and desires. Portraits of newly rich merchants were commissioned, as were paintings of weddings and famous battles.

The revolution in art began in Florence, where the merchant class, flush with profits from trading and banking, began commissioning art. Prior to this, the church had been the main sponsor of art and the works it commissioned reflected medieval beliefs. The merchant class, who had fought so hard to overcome the restrictive class system of the Middle Ages, was more open to innovation. Florence, one of the wealthiest city-states, helped launch this new artistic attitude through four of its artistic geniuses. Florentine Giotto's (1276–1336) use of realism inspired many artists after him. Masaccio (1402–1429?), introduced three-dimensional perspective into painting. Fra Filippo Lippi (1406–1469), a priest, expressed humanism by painting Florentine citizens in scenes of the Holy Family. Sandro Botticelli (1447–1510) continued this concept by portraying his sponsors, the powerful Medici family, in his *Adoration of the Magi.*

At first, the guardians of medieval tradition—the Holy Roman Church—persecuted some artists for their audacity. Any deviation from traditional subject matter or techniques could be cause to haul the artist before a tribunal, forcing the artist to destroy or change his work. By the sixteenth century even the church recognized the unparalleled talents of these new artists, and became a major patron to many of them, sponsoring some of the greatest works to emerge from the Renaissance. For example, Florentine Leonardo da Vinci (1452–1519), whose genius as an inventor, scientist, and architect rivaled his accomplishments as an artist, produced the *Mona Lisa* and the *Last Supper,* considered masterworks of the Renaissance.

While the visual and performing arts such as painting, sculpture, architecture, and music were as accessible to the illiterate as to the literate, literature faced the challenge of appealing to the much smaller group of people who could read. Toward this end, Renaissance writers abandoned writing poetry and prose exclusively in Greek and Latin and began writing in their native languages. The growing literacy of the middle class, prompted by a healthy economy and the invention of the printing press, helped popularize literature, and Renaissance writers consciously wrote to their new readership. As with the visual arts, the subject matter of writers became more secular, bawdy, and humorous, including subjects such as love, chivalry, and adventure. Books which before might have been appreciated by only a few of the elite were now read and discussed in taverns and shops throughout Europe.

To the Detractors of Poetry

Giovanni Boccaccio

Born in France but of an Italian family, Giovanni Boccaccio (1313–1375) was, along with his friend Petrarch (1304–1374), one of the primary architects of the Renaissance. As a writer, Boccaccio is famous today for his bawdy fictional tales in the *Decameron*, considered to be a masterpiece of Italian classic prose and an enormous influence on Renaissance literature throughout Europe. However, perhaps even of greater influence on the Renaissance was his scholarship and commentaries on the ancient Greek and Roman writings that made popular the Humanism that would be embraced by subsequent Renaissance figures and come to define that age. He also helped popularize literature of his own time, elevating it in status to equal the classics.

The following passage is from *Genealogia Deorum Gentilium* (*On the Genealogy of the Gods of the Gentiles*), Boccaccio's encyclopedic collection of classical myth, which he began about the same time he met Petrarch, in 1350, and continually revised for the next twenty-five years until his death. It is this and similar scholarly works, and not the "vulgar" *Decameron,* for which he wanted to be remembered. In this defense of poetry, he describes it as a positive force in exalting God and the Catholic religion. In an Italy infested by war, famine, greed, and selfish ambition, leaders guided by a poetic vision of purity would rise to restore the society to greatness.

Excerpted from "The Author Addresses the Enemies of Poetry in Hope of Their Reform," by Giovanni Boccaccio, *Boccaccio on Poetry*, edited by Charles G. Osgood (New York: Liberal Arts Press, 1930).

A nd now, O men of sense, ye will do wisely to calm your indignation and quiet your swollen hearts. Our contest has grown perhaps too bitter. You began by taking up the cudgel against an innocent class of men, with the intention of exterminating them. I came to their defence, and, with God's help and the merits of the case, did what I could to save deserving men from their deadly enemies. Yet, if the poets in person had fairly taken the field against you, you would see how far their powers surpass both yours and mine, and repent at the eleventh hour. But the fight is over; with some glory of war, and a good deal more sweat, we have reached the point where the lust for victory may be a bit qualified, and we may part company with a fair settlement. Come then, let us freely unite to rest from our labors, for the prizes of the contest have been awarded. You forfeit to me your theory, and I to you a bit of consolation; this leaves ample room for peace. I have no doubt you are willing, since you are sorry to have begun the contest, and by this arrangement we shall both enjoy its benefits. To prove my sincerity, I, who am the first to tire of it, will be the first to resume friendly relations; that you may do likewise, I beg of you to consider with fair and unruffled mind the few words which I, in all charity and friendship, am about to say to you.

Hidden Meanings in Poetry

You recall, gentlemen, that, as well as I could, I have shown you the nature of poetry, which you had counted as naught, who the poets are, their function, and their manner of life, whom you cried out upon as depraved liars, moral perverters, corrupt with a thousand evils. I have shown also the nature of the Muses, whom you had called drabs and consigned to the stews. Yet being actually so worthy of regard as I have shown, you should not only cease to condemn them, but should cherish, magnify, love them, and search their books to your improvement. And that old age may not prevent you, or the popularity of other arts, try your best to do what an aged prince was not ashamed to attempt; I refer to that shining example of all virtues, famous [fourteenth-century monarch] King Robert of Sicily and Jerusalem, who besides being king, was a distinguished philosopher, an eminent teacher of medicine, and an exceptional theologian in his day. Yet in his sixty-sixth year he retained a contempt for [first-century B.C. Roman poet] Vergil, and, like you, called him and the rest mere story-tellers, and of no value at all apart from the ornament of his verse. But as soon as he heard Petrarch unfold the hidden meaning of his poetry, he was struck with amazement, and saw and rejected his own error; and I actually heard him say that he never had supposed such great and lofty meaning could lie hidden under so flimsy a cover of poetic fiction as he now saw revealed through the demonstration of this expert critic. With wonderfully keen regret he began upbraiding his own judgment and his misfortune in recognizing so late the true art of poetry. Neither fear of criticism, nor age, nor the sense of his fast expiring lease of life were enough to prevent him from abandoning his studies in the other great sciences and arts, and devoting himself to the mastery of Vergil's meaning. As it happened, an early end broke off his new pursuit, but if he might have continued in it, without doubt he would have won much glory for the poets, and no little advantage for the Italians engaged in such studies. Will you, then, hold that gift not worth the taking which was holy in the sight of this wise king? Impossible! You are not mere tigers or huge beasts, whose minds, like their ferocity, cannot be turned to better account.

Good Poets Bring Harmony

But if my pious expectation is doomed to disappointment, and the heat of your hatred still burns against them who deserve it not, then whenever your tongues itch to be at it again, I beseech you, for the sake of your own decency, mind my words. I adjure you, by the sacred breast of Philosophy, which haply in other days has nourished you, not to rush in headlong fury upon the whole company of poets. Rather, if you have sense enough, you must observe right and timely distinction among them—such distinction as only can bring harmony out of discord, dispel the clouds of ignorance, clear the understanding, and set the mind in the right way. This you must do if you would not confuse the poets we revere—many of them pagans, as I have shown—with the disreputable sort. Let the lewd comic writers [those who wrote only for money, exploiting human weakness for ridicule rather than enlightenment] feel the stream of your wrath, the fiery blast of your eloquence; but be content to leave the rest in peace. Spare also the Hebrew authors. Them you cannot rend without insulting God's majesty itself. I have already cited [fifth-century Roman biblical scholar Saint] Jerome's statement that some of them uttered their prophetic song in poetic style as dictated by the Holy Ghost. By the same token must Christian writers escape injury; for many even of our own tongue have been poets—nay, still survive—who, under cover of their compositions, have expressed the deep and holy meaning of Christianity. One of many instances is our [fourteenth-century Italian poet] Dante [Alighieri]. True, he wrote in his mother tongue [Italian], which he adapted to his artistic purpose; yet in the book which he called the *Commedia* he nobly described the three-fold condition of departed souls consistently with the sacred teaching of theology. The famous modern poet Petrarch has, in his *Bucolics*, employed the pastoral guise to show forth with marvellous effect both the praise and the blame visited by the true God and the glorious Trinity upon the idle ship of Peter. Many such volumes are there which yield their meaning to any zealous inquirer. Such are the poems of [fourth-century Christian poet Aurelius Clemens] Pruden-tius, and [fifth-century Christian poet] Sedulius, which express sacred truth in disguise. [Sixth-century Christian poet] Arator, who was not merely a Christian, but a priest and car-dinal in the church of Rome, gave poetic form to the Acts of the Apostles by recounting them in heroics. [Fourth-century Christian poet] Juvencus, the Spaniard, also a Christian, em-ployed the symbolic device of the man, the ox, the lion, and the eagle, to describe all the acts of Christ our Redeemer,

Son of the Living God. Without citing further examples, let me say that, if no consideration of gentleness can induce you to spare poets of our own nation, yet be not more severe than our mother the Church; for she, with laudable regard, does not scorn to favor many a writer; but especially hath she honored [second-century Christian theologian] Origen. So great was his power in composition that his mind seemed inexhaustible and his hand tireless; so much so that the number of his treatises on various subjects is thought to have reached a thousand. But the Church is like the wise maiden who gathered flowers among thorns without tearing her fingers, simply by leaving the thorns untouched; so she has rejected the less trustworthy part of Origen, and retained the deserving part to be laid up among her treasures. Therefore distinguish with care, weigh the words of the poets in a true balance, and put away the unholy part. Neither condemn what is excellent, as if, by raising a sudden hue and cry against poets, you hoped to seem Augustines [fifth-century Christian theologian St. Augustine of Hippo] or Jeromes to an ignorant public. They were men whose wisdom equalled their righteousness; they directed their attack not against poetry, or the art of poetry, but against the pagan errors contained in the poet's works. At these they hurled fearless and outspoken condemnation because it was a time when Catholic truth was surrounded and beset with harassing enemies. At the same time they cherished them and ever recognized in these works so much art, and polish, such seasoning of wisdom and skilful application of ornament, that whoever would acquire any grace of Latin style apparently must derive it from them.

Finally in the words of [second-century B.C. Roman statesman Marcus Tullius] Cicero pleading for [second-century B.C. Greek poet Aulus Licinius] Archias: [charged with illegally assuming the rights of a Roman citizen] "These studies may engage the strength of our manhood and divert us in old age; they are the adornment of prosperity, the refuge and solace of adversity; delightful at home, convenient in all places; they are ever with us through the night season; in our travels; in our rural retreats. And if we may not pursue them ourselves nor enjoy them in person, yet should we admire them as seen in others," etc. Poetry, then, and poets too, should be cultivated, not spurned and rejected; and if you are wise enough to realize this there is nothing more to say. On the other hand, if you persevere in your obstinate madness, though I feel sorry for you, contemptible as you are, yet no writing in the world could help you.

The Superiority of Visual Art

Leonardo da Vinci

No person has come to represent the ideal of the multi-faceted Renaissance Man more than Italian Leonardo da Vinci (1452–1519). In an era filled with men and women of extraordinary accomplishments in many fields, his list of achievements leaves all the others far behind. He was a painter, sculptor, musician, ornithologist, anatomist, meteorologist, architect, mathematician, engineer, inventor, and more. His most famous paintings include the *Mona Lisa* and the *Last Supper*, while his numerous inventions include the bicycle, pedometer, magnifying glass, alarm clock, gas mask, life preserver, and submarine. So dedicated was he to the study of anatomy, both for the advancement of science and for his art studies, that he was banished from Rome by the pope for refusing to stop dissecting cadavers.

Although self-described as illiterate, he filled many notebooks with his writings about nature, science, and art. The following passages illustrate his most important belief, that the eyes were the most important means to acquiring knowledge. But one had to be taught how to see properly, which he sets about doing in his writings on art.

He who despises painting loves neither philosophy nor nature

If you scorn painting, which is the sole imitator of all the manifest works of nature, you will certainly be scorning a

Excerpted from *Leonardo on Painting*, by Leonardo da Vinci, edited by Martin Kemp, translated by Martin Kemp and Margaret Walker (New Haven, CT: Yale University Press, 1989). Copyright © 1989 by Yale University Press. Reprinted with permission.

subtle invention, which with philosophical and subtle spec-ulation considers all manner of forms: sea, land, trees, ani-mals, grasses, flowers, all of which are enveloped in light and shade. Truly this is science, the legitimate daughter of nature, because painting is born of that nature; but to be more correct, we should say the granddaughter of nature, because all visible things have been brought forth by nature and it is among these that painting is born. Therefore we may justly speak of it as the granddaughter of nature and as the kin of god.

Why painting is not numbered amongst the sciences

Because writers had no access to definitions of the sci-ence of painting, they were not able to describe its rank and constituent elements. Since painting does not achieve its ends through words, it is placed below the . . . sciences through ignorance, but it does not on this account lose its di-vinity. And in truth it is not difficult to understand why it has not been accorded nobility, because it possesses nobility in itself without the help of the tongues of others—no less than do the excellent works of nature. If the painters have not de-scribed and codified their art as science, it is not the fault of painting, and it is none the less noble for that. Few painters make a profession of writing since their life is too short for its cultivation. Would we similarly deny the existence of the particular qualities of herbs, stones or plants because men were not acquainted with them? Certainly not. We should say that these herbs retained their intrinsic nobility, without the help of human language or writings.

Whether painting is a science or not

That mental discourse that originates in first principles is termed science. Nothing can be found in nature that is not part of science, like continuous quantity, that is to say, geometry, which, commencing with the surfaces of bodies, is found to have its origins in lines, the boundary of these surfaces. Yet we do not remain satisfied with this, in that we know that line has its conclusion in a point, and nothing can be smaller than that which is a point. Therefore the point is the first principle of geometry, and no other thing can be found either in nature or in the human mind that can give rise to the point. . . .

No human investigation may claim to be a true science if it has not passed through mathematical demonstrations, and if you say that the sciences that begin and end in the mind exhibit truth, this cannot be allowed, but must be denied for many reasons, above all because such mental discourses do not involve experience, without which nothing can be achieved with certainty.

Those sciences are termed mathematical which, passing through the senses, are certain to the highest degree, and these are only two in number. The first is arithmetic and the second geometry, one dealing with discontinuous quantity and the other with continuous quantity. From these is born perspective, devoted to all the functions of the eye and to its delight with various speculations. From these three, arithmetic, geometry and perspective—and if one of them is missing nothing can be accomplished—astronomy arises by means of the visual rays. With number and measure it calculates the distances and dimensions of the heavenly bodies, as well as the terrestrial ones. Next comes music, which is born of continuous and discrete quantities and which is dedicated to the ear, a sense less noble than the eye. Through the ear, music sends the various harmonies of diverse instruments to the *sensus communis* [Latin phrase referring to location in brain where medieval scientists believed the nerves from each of the five senses converged to be correlated]. Next follows smell, which satisfies the *sensus communis* with various odours, but although these odours give rise to fragrance, a harmony similar to music, none the less it is not in man's power to make a science out of it. The same applies to taste and touch. . . .

What is the first intentional aim of the painter?

The first intention of the painter is to make a flat surface display a body as if modelled and separated from this plane, and he who most surpasses others in this skill deserves most praise. This accomplishment, with which the science of painting is crowned, arises from light and shade, or we may say *chiaroscuro*. Therefore, whoever fights shy of shadow fights shy of the glory of art as recognised by noble intellects, but acquires glory according to the ignorant masses, who require nothing of painting other than beauty of colour, totally forgetting the beauty and wonder of a flat surface displaying relief.

There are two principal parts into which painting is divided: firstly the outlines which surround the shapes of solid bodies—and these outlines require draughtsmanship; and secondly what is called shading. But draughtsmanship is of such excellence that it not only investigates the works of nature but also infinitely more than those made by nature. . . . On this account we should conclude that it is not only a science but a goddess which should be duly accorded that title. This deity repeats all the visible works of almighty God. . . .

How painting surpasses all the works of man on account of the subtle speculations with which it is concerned

The eye, which is said to be the window of the soul, is the primary means by which the *sensus communis* of the brain may most fully and magnificently contemplate the infinite works of nature, and the ear is the second, acquiring nobility through the recounting of things which the eye has seen. If you, historians or poets or mathematicians, had not seen things through your eyes, you would only be able to report them feebly in your writings. And you, poet, should you wish to depict a story as if painting with your pen, the painter with his brush will more likely succeed and will be understood less laboriously. If you assert that painting is dumb poetry, then the painter may call poetry blind painting. It may be said, therefore, that poetry is the science that serves as the pre-eminent medium for the blind, and painting does the same for the deaf. But painting remains the worthier in as much as it serves the nobler sense and remakes the forms and figures of nature with greater truth than the poet. And the works of nature are far more worthy than words, which are the products of man, because there is the same relationship between the works of man and those of nature as between man and god. Therefore, it is nobler to

Art on Trial

Popular Italian artist Paolo Veronese (1528–1588) was renowned for his brilliant use of color and his large, vastly peopled paintings depicting allegorical, biblical, and historical settings. As a result, he was commissioned to do many religious works at various churches. However, in 1573, the Holy Office of the Venetian Inquisition summoned Veronese to defend his painting, the Last Supper, *for its use of irreverent elements. His defense of artistic freedom is all the more admirable considering his judges had the power of imprisonment and worse.*

Inquisitor's question: What picture is this of which you have spoken?

Veronese's answer: This is a picture of the Last Supper that Jesus Christ took with His Apostles in the house of Simon. . . .

Q. At this Supper of Our Lord have you painted other figures?

A. Yes, milords. . . .

Q. What is the significance of those armed men dressed as Germans, each with a halberd in his hand? . . .

A. We painters take the same license the poets and the jesters take and I have represented these two halberdiers, one drinking and the other eating nearby on the stairs. They are placed here so that they might be of service because it seemed to me fitting, according to what I have been told, that the mater of the house, who was great and rich, should have such servants.

Q. And that man dressed as a buffoon with a parrot on his wrist, for what purpose did you paint him on that canvas?

A. For ornament, as is customary. . . .

Q. Who do you really believe was present at that Supper?

A. I believe one would find Christ with His Apostles. But if in a picture there is some space to spare I enrich it with figures according to the stories. . . .

Q. Are not the decorations . . . supposed to be suitable and proper to the subject and the principal figures or are they for pleasure—simply what comes to your imagination without any discretion or judiciousness?

A. I paint pictures as I see fit and as well as my talent permits.

Q. Does it seem fitting at the Last Supper of the Lord to paint buffoons, drunkards, Germans, dwarfs and similar vulgarities?

A. No, milords. . . .

Q. Do you not know that in Germany and in other places infected with heresy it is customary with various pictures full of scurrilousness and similar inventions to mock, vituperate, and scorn the things of the Holy Catholic Church in order to teach bad doctrines to foolish and ignorant people?

A. Yes that is wrong; but I return to what I have said, that I am obliged to follow what my superiors have done.

Q. What have your superiors done? Have they perhaps done similar things?

A. Michelangelo in Rome in the Pontifical Chapel painted our Lord, Jesus Christ, His Mother, St. John, St. Peter, and the Heavenly Host. These are all represented in the nude—even the Virgin Mary—and in different poses with little reverence.

Q. Do you not know that in painting the Last Judgment in which no garments or similar things are presumed, it was not necessary to paint garments, and that in those figures there is nothing that is not spiritual? There are neither buffoons, dogs, weapons, or similar buffoonery. And does it seem because of this or some other example that you did right to have painted this picture in the way you did and do you want to maintain that it is good and decent?

A. Illustrious Lords, I do not want to defend it, but I thought I was doing right. I did not consider so many things and I did not intend to confuse anyone, the more so as those figures of buffoons are outside of the place in a picture where Our Lord is represented.

[After these things had been said, the judges announced that the above named Paolo would be obliged to improve and change his painting within a period of three months . . . and that according to the opinion and decision of the Holy Tribunal all the corrections should be made at the expense of the painter and that if he did not correct the picture he would be liable to the penalties imposed by the Holy Tribunal.]

Kenneth J. Atchity, ed., *The Renaissance Reader.* New York: HarperPerennial, 1997.

imitate things in nature, which are in fact the real images, than to imitate, in words, the words and deeds of man.

Now, do you not see that the eye embraces the beauty of all the world? The eye is the commander of astronomy; it makes cosmography; it guides and rectifies all the human arts; it conducts man to the various regions of this world; it is the prince of mathematics; its sciences are most certain; it has measured the height and size of the stars; it has disclosed the elements and their distributions; it has made predictions of future events by means of the course of the stars; it has generated architecture, perspective and divine painting. Oh excellent above all other things created by God! What manner of praises could match your nobility? What races, what languages would they be that could describe in full your functions . . . ? Using the eye, human industry has discovered fire, by which means it is able to regain what darkness had previously taken away. It has graced nature with agriculture and delectable gardens.

But what need is there for me to expand into an elevated and lengthy discourse? What is there that cannot be accomplished by the eye? It allows men to move from east to west. It has discovered navigation. And it triumphs over nature, in that the constituent parts of nature are finite, but the works which the eye commands of the hands are infinite, as is demonstrated by the painter in his rendering of numberless forms of animals, grasses, trees and places. . . .

The difference between painting and poetry

The imagination cannot see with such excellence as the eye, because the eye receives and gives the images or rather the semblances of the objects to the *imprensiva* [Leonardo's own term for a "receptor of impressions"], and from this *imprensiva* to the *sensus communis,* where it is interpreted, but the imagination is unable to exist outside the *sensus communis,* unless it passes to the memory where it terminates and dies if the thing imagined is not of great excellence. Poetry arises in the mind and imagination of the poet, who desires to depict the same things as the painter. He wishes to parallel the painter, but in truth he is far removed. . . . Therefore, with respect to representation, we may justly claim that the difference between the science of painting and poetry is equivalent to that between a body and its cast shadow. And yet the difference is even greater than this, because the shadow of the body at least enters the *sensus communis* through the eye, while the imagined form of the body does not enter through this sense, but is born in the darkness of the inner eye. Oh! what a difference there is between the imaginary quality of such light in the dark inner eye and actually seeing it outside this darkness!

Painting immediately presents to you the demonstrations which its maker has intended and gives as much pleasure to the greatest of senses as anything created by nature. And in this case, the poet who sends the same thing to the *sensus communis* via hearing, a lesser sense, cannot give any greater pleasure to the eye than if you were listening to something spoken. Now, see what difference there is between hearing an extended account of something that pleases the eye and seeing it instantaneously, just as natural things are seen. Yet the works of the poets must be read over a long span of time. Often there are occasions when they are not understood and it is necessary to compose various commentaries, and very rarely do the commentators understand what was intended by the mind of the poet. And many times authors do not read out any more than a small part of their work through lack of time. But the work of the painter is instantaneously accessible to his spectators.

Painting presents its essence to you in one moment through the faculty of vision by the same means as the *imprensiva* receives the objects in nature, and thus it simultaneously conveys the proportional harmony of which the parts of the whole are composed, and delights the senses. Poetry presents the same thing but by a less noble means than by the eye, conveying it more confusedly to the *imprensiva* and describing the configurations of the particular objects more slowly than is accomplished by the eye. The eye is the true intermediary between the objects and the *imprensiva,* which immediately transmits with the highest fidelity the true surfaces and shapes of whatever is in front of it. And from these is born the proportionality called harmony, which delights the sense with sweet concord, no differently from the proportionality made by different musical notes to the sense of hearing. And yet hearing is less noble than sight, in that as it is born so it dies, and it is as fleeting in its death as it is in its birth. This cannot apply to the sense of sight, because if you represent to the eye a human beauty composed of proportionately beautiful parts, this beauty will not be so impermanent or rapidly destroyed as that made by music. On the contrary, it has great permanence and allows you to see and contemplate it, and does not need to be reborn in numerous performances like music, nor will it induce boredom in you. Rather, human beauty will stimulate love in you, and will make all your senses envious, as if they wished to emulate the eye—as if the mouth would wish to suck it into the body, as if the ear would seek its pleasure from being able to hear visual beauty, as if the sense of touch would wish it to be infused through the pores, and as if the nose would wish to inhale it with the air that it continually exhales.

If you were to say that poetry is more enduring, I would reply that the works of a coppersmith are even more enduring, because time conserves them better than the works of both of us. Nevertheless, the coppersmith requires little imagination. And by painting with enamels on copper, pictures can be made more durable. Time will destroy the harmony of human beauty in a few years, but this does not occur with such beauty imitated by the painter, because time will long preserve it. And the eye, in keeping with its function, will derive as much true pleasure from depicted beauty as from the living beauty denied to it. . . . In this case, the painted imitation can provide a surrogate in large measure—a form of substitution that the poet cannot effect. In such matters the poet may wish to rival the painter, but he does not allow for the fact that the words with which he delineates the elements of beauty are separated from one another by time, which leaves voids between them and dismembers the proportions. He cannot delineate them without excessive wordiness, and not being able to depict them, he cannot compose the proportional harmonies that are produced by divine proportions. During the very time that it takes to embrace the contemplation of painted beauty it is not possible to accomplish a beautiful description, and it is a sin against nature to send via the ear those things that should be sent via the eye. Let the effects of music enter through the ear, but do not send the science of painting that way, since it is the true imitator of the natural shapes of all things.

A poem, which has to accomplish the representation of a given beauty by means of the representation of each of those parts which would comprise the same harmony in a painting, does not achieve any more grace than music would produce if each note were to be heard on its own at various intervals, failing to produce any harmony—just as if you wished to show a face part by part, always covering the section previously shown. In such a demonstration, the concealment does not allow the composition of any proportional harmony because the eye cannot embrace all of it within its faculty of vision simultaneously.

Michelangelo Paints the Sistine Chapel

Ascanio Condivi

Minor Italian artist Ascanio Condivi (1525?–1574) was a young assistant and pupil of the great Italian Renaissance artist Michelangelo Buonarroti (1475–1564). The closeness of their relationship allowed Condivi access to the master's most personal thoughts, making his biography, *The Life of Michel-Angelo*, excerpted below, the most intimate portrait available.

So influential was the art of Michelangelo that some historians credit him with being responsible, directly and indirectly, for three separate historical eras. The word Renaissance was said to be specifically created to describe the development of fine arts under Michelangelo and fellow artist Raphael (1483–1520). The Reformation was spurred by Martin Luther's (1483–1546) rejection of the Catholic Church's sale of indulgences (by which sins are forgiven by God). The sale of indulgences increased dramatically when Pope Julius II (1443–1513) needed money to pay for his own elaborate tomb, to be created by Michelangelo. The Baroque era (1600–1750) in art is characterized by figures who display emotions appropriate to the circumstances, a movement which some claim was inspired by Michelangelo's figures from his painting of the ceiling of the Sistine Chapel.

The painting of the Sistine Chapel is one of the most dramatic events in art history, not just because the results were so magnificent, but because the task proved so challenging. Michelangelo was required to lie flat on his back for many hours at a time over a period of several years. Though he began the arduous task in 1508, the work was not completed until 1512. In 1534, he was appointed official sculptor, painter, and architect for the Vatican. During this time he painted *The Last Judgment*, inspired, in part, by his own fears of being judged unworthy by God. This theme of self-doubt reoccurs in his poetry, which is also considered to be among the finest of the Italian Renaissance. In his poems he refers to art as a "false idol" that took time away from what he should have been doing, meditating on God.

When Michelangelo had finished this work, he came on to Rome, where [sixteenth-century papal art patron] Pope Julius, still resolved not to do the tomb, was anxious to employ him. Then [sixteenth-century Italian architect Donato] Bramante and other rivals of Michelangelo put it into the pope's head that he should have Michelangelo paint the vault of the chapel of [fifteenth-century papal leader] Pope Sixtus IV, which is in the palace, raising hopes that in this he would accomplish miracles. And they were doing this service with malice, in order to distract the pope from projects of sculpture, and because they took it for certain that either he would turn the pope against him by not accepting such an undertaking or, if he accepted it, he would prove considerably inferior to [sixteenth-century Italian painter and architect] Raphael of Urbino, whom they plied with every favor out of hatred for Michelangelo, as it was their opinion that Michelangelo's principal art was the making of statues (as indeed it was). Michelangelo, who had not yet used colors and who realized that it was difficult to paint a vault, made every effort to get out of it, proposing Raphael and pleading that this was not his art and that he would not succeed; and he went on refusing to such an extent that the pope almost lost his temper. But, when he saw that the pope was determined, he embarked on that work which is to be seen today in the papal palace to the admiration and amazement of the world, and which brought him so great a reputation that it set him above all envy. Of this work I shall give a brief account. . . .

At the head of the chapel, then, in the first space, which

is one of the smaller ones, God the Almighty is to be seen
in the heavens, dividing light from darkness by the motion
of His arms. In the second space is the creation of the two
great lights, in which He appears with arms outstretched,
with His right arm pointing toward the sun and His left toward the moon. There are some little angels in His company,
one of whom at His left side hides his face and draws close
to his Creator as if to protect himself from the evil influence
of the moon. In this same space, at the left side, God appears
again, turning to create the grasses and the plants on earth,
executed with such great artistry that, wherever you turn, He
seems to follow you, showing His whole back down to the
soles of His feet, a very beautiful thing, which demonstrates
what foreshortening [portraying an object with the apparent
shortening due to visual perspective] can do. In the third
space, the great God appears in the heavens, again with angels, and gazes upon the water, commanding them to bring
forth all the species of creatures which that element sustains,
just as in the second space He commanded the earth. In the
fourth is *The Creation of Man,* where God is seen with arm
and hand outstretched as if to impart to Adam the precepts
as to what he must and must not do, while with the other
arm He gathers His little angels around Him. In the fifth is
when He draws woman from Adam's rib and she, rising
with hands joined and held out toward God and bowing in
an attitude of meekness, seems to be thanking Him and He
to be blessing her. In the sixth is when the devil, in human
form from the waist up and the rest in that of a serpent, with
his legs transformed into tails, coils around a tree and, pre-
tending to reason with the man, persuades him to act against
his Creator while to the woman he proffers the forbidden ap-
ple. And the other part of the space shows them both, expelled by the angel, stricken with fear and grief, fleeing
from the face of God.

  In the seventh is the sacrifice of Abel and Cain, the one
pleasing and acceptable to God, the other abhorrent and rejected. In the eighth is *The Flood,* in which Noah's ark can
be seen in the distance, in the midst of the waters, with some

figures who are clinging to it to be saved. Nearer, in the same sea, there is a boat laden with various people, which, because it is overloaded and because of the frequent and violent shocks of the waves, its sail lost, bereft of all aid or human remedy, is already shipping water and going down. Here it is pitiful to see the human race perish so miserably in the waves. Likewise, nearer the eye, a mountaintop appears still above the waters, like an island, to which a multitude of men and women have retreated as they flee the rising waters; they express various emotions, but all pathetic and fearful, as they draw under a tent stretched over a tree for protection against the extraordinary rain; and, overhead, the wrath of God is represented with great artistry, pouring down upon them with waters, with thunder, and with lightning. There is another mountain peak at the right side, considerably nearer the eye, with a multitude ravaged by the same disaster, whose every detail would take a long time to describe; suffice it to say that they are all lifelike and awesome, as one might imagine in such a calamity. In the ninth, which is the last, is the story of Noah when he lay drunk on the ground with his privy parts exposed and was derided by his son Ham and covered by Shem and Japheth. . . .

In all these things, in the beauty of the compartments, in the diversity of poses, in the contradiction of the contours of the vault, Michelangelo displayed consummate art. But, to relate the details of these and the other things would be an endless undertaking, and a volume would not suffice. Therefore I have passed over it briefly, wishing merely to cast a little light on the whole rather than to go into detail as to the parts.

Anxieties on the Job

And, in the midst of all this, he was not without anxieties because, when he had begun the work and completed the picture of *The Flood,* it began to mildew so that the figures could barely be distinguished. Therefore Michelangelo, reckoning that this must be a sufficient excuse for him to escape such a burden, went to the pope and said to him, "Indeed I told Your Holiness that this is not my art; what I have done is spoiled. And if you do not believe it, send someone to see." The pope sent San Gallo, who, when he saw it, realized that Michelangelo had applied the plaster too wet, and consequently the dampness coming through produced that effect; and, when Michelangelo had been advised of this, he was forced to continue, and no excuse served.

While he was painting, Pope Julius often wanted to go and inspect the work; he would climb up by a ladder and Michelangelo would hold out a hand to him to help him up onto the scaffolding. And, being one who was by nature impetuous and impatient of waiting, as soon as the work was half done, that is from the door to midway on the vault, he wanted Michelangelo to uncover it while it was still incomplete and had not received the final coat. The opinion and the expectation which everyone had of Michelangelo brought all of Rome to see this thing, and the pope also went there before the dust raised by the dismantling of the scaffold had settled.

After this work, when Raphael had seen the new and wonderful manner of painting, as he had a remarkable gift for imitation, he sought through Bramante to paint the rest himself. This greatly disturbed Michelangelo, and before Pope Julius he gravely protested the wrong which Bramante was doing him; and in Bramante's presence he complained to the pope, unfolding to him all the persecutions he had received from Bramante; and next he exposed many of his deficiencies, and mainly that, in demolishing the old St. Peter's, Bramante was pulling down those marvelous columns which were in that temple, with no regard or concern for their being broken to pieces, when he could lower them gently and preserve them intact; and he explained that it was easy to put one brick on top of another, but that to make such a column was extremely difficult, and many other things which need not be told, so that, when the pope had heard of these derelictions, he wanted Michelangelo to continue, conferring upon him more favors than ever. He finished this entire work in twenty months, without any help whatever, not even someone to grind his colors for him. It is true that I have heard him say that it is not finished as he would have wanted, as he was hampered by the urgency of the pope, who asked him one day when he would finish that chapel, and when Michelangelo answered, "When I can," the pope, enraged, retorted, "You want me to have you thrown off the scaffolding." Hearing this, Michelangelo said to himself, "You shall not have me thrown off," and he removed himself and had the scaffolding taken down, and on All Saints' Day he revealed the work, which the pope, who went to the chapel that day, saw with immense satisfaction, and all Rome admired it and crowded to see it. What was lacking was the retouching of the work *a secco* [painting on dry plaster with pigments mixed in water] with ultramarine and in a few places with gold, to give it a richer appearance. Julius, when the heat of his enthusiasm had subsided, really wanted Michelangelo to furnish these touches; but, when Michelangelo thought about the trouble it would give him to reassemble the scaffolding, he answered that what was lacking was nothing of importance. "It really ought to be retouched with gold," answered the pope, to whom Michelangelo responded with the familiarity which was his way with His Holiness, "I do not see that men wear gold." The pope said, "It will look poor." Michelangelo rejoined, "Those who are depicted there, they were poor too." So he remarked in jest, and so the work has remained.

For this work and for all his expenses, Michelangelo received three thousand ducats [a gold coin once in use throughout Europe], of which he was obliged to spend about twenty or twenty-five on colors, according to what I have heard him say. After he had accomplished this work, because he had spent such a long time painting with his eyes looking up at the vault, Michelangelo then could not see much when he looked down; so that, if he had to read a letter or other detailed things, he had to hold them with his arms up over his head. Nonetheless, after a while, he gradually grew accustomed to reading again with his eyes looking down. From this we may conceive how great were the attention and diligence with which he did this work.

Defense of Poesy

Philip Sidney

The Renaissance spirit was not just about becoming learned and successful in as many fields as possible, it was also about using one's knowledge and abilities to improve the world. Self-interest and self-indulgence were replaced by self-sacrifice in the pursuit of a better world. England's Sir Philip Sidney (1554–1586) embodied this spirit of idealism. As a politician, military leader, and poet, he actively involved himself in the betterment of England in every area. While a member of Parliament, he encouraged exploration of the Americas and hosted many foreign dignitaries. He was also a patron of many scholars and writers, resulting in more than forty works by European and English writers dedicated to him. However, Sidney desired a more adventurous life, which led him to volunteer to fight against the Spanish. At the age of thirty-one, he died of wounds received in battle.

One of the best English poets of his time, Sidney composed a series of love sonnets, *Astrophel and Stella*, the first such sequence to be written in English. When poetry came under attack by some Puritans as being immoral and frivolous, he turned his attention to writing *Defense of Poesy*, excerpted below, considered the best work of literary criticism from the entire Elizabethan era (that is, during the reign of England's Queen Elizabeth, 1558–1603). In it he eloquently presents a case for the importance of imaginative writing to society, showing how the great writers of other disciplines, such as history, philosophy, and religion, borrowed or stole from poetry in order to be more effective communicators.

Excerpted from *Defense of Poesy*, by Sir Philip Sidney, edited by Dorothy M. Macardle (London: Macmillan & Co. Ltd., 1919).

And yet I must say that, as I have just cause to make a pitiful defence of poor poetry, which from almost the highest estimation of learning is fallen to be the laughing-stock of children, so have I need to bring some more available proofs, sith [since] the former [refers to learning] is by no man barred of his deserved credit, the silly [simple] latter [meaning poetry] hath had even the names of philosophers used to the defacing of it, with great danger of civil war among the Muses [in Greek and Roman mythology, nine goddesses who inspire people to create artistic expressions].

A History of Noble Poets

And first, truly, to all them that, professing learning, inveigh against poetry, may justly be objected that they go very near to ungratefulness, to seek to deface that which, in the noblest nations and languages that are known, hath been the first light-giver to ignorance, and first nurse, whose milk by little and little enabled them to feed afterwards of tougher knowledges. And will they now play the hedgehog, that, being received into the den, drave out his host? Or rather the vipers, that with their birth kill their parents? Let learned Greece in any of her manifold sciences be able to show me one book before Musaeus [in Greek mythology a minor deity and poet], [ninth-century B.C. Greek poet] Homer, and [ninth-century B.C. Greek poet] Hesiod, all three nothing else but poets. Nay, let any history be brought that can say any writers were there before them, if they were not men of the same skill, as Orpheus [in Greek mythology a musician with supernatural skills], Linus [in Greek mythology a great musician], and some other are named, who, having been the first of that country that made pens deliverers of their knowledge to their posterity, may justly challenge to be called their fathers in learning. For not only in time they had this priority (although in itself antiquity be venerable) but went before them as causes, to draw with their charming sweetness the wild untamed wits to an admiration of knowledge. So as Amphion [in Greek mythology a great singer and musician whose music causes the stones around Thebes to form a protective wall] was said to move stones with his poetry to build [major ancient Greek city] Thebes, and Orpheus to be listened to by beasts, indeed stony and beastly people. So among the Romans were [third-century B.C. Greek writer] Livius Andronicus and [second-century B.C. Greek poet Quintus] Ennius; so in the Italian language the first that made it aspire to be a treasure-house of science were the poets [fourteenth-century Italian poet] Dante [Alighieri], [fourteenth-century Italian poet Giovanni] Boccace [Boccaccio], and [fourteenth-century Italian poet Francesco] Petrarch; so in our English were [fourteenth-century English poet John] Gower and [fourteenth-century Italian poet Geoffrey] Chaucer, after whom, encouraged and delighted with their excellent foregoing, others have followed to beautify our mother-tongue, as well in the same kind as in other arts.

This did so notably show itself, that the philosophers of Greece durst not a long time appear to the world but under the masks of poets. So [sixth-century B.C. Greek philosopher] Thales [of Miletus], [fifth-century B.C. Greek poet] Empedocles, and [sixth-century B.C. Greek poet] Parmenides sang their natural philosophy in verses; so did [sixth-century B.C. Greek mathematician and philosopher] Pythagoras and [sixth-century B.C. Greek poet] Phocylides their moral counsels; so did [seventh-century B.C. Greek poet of military verse] Tyrtaeus in war matters, and [sixth-century B.C. Greek poet] Solon in matters of policy; or rather they, being poets, did exercise their delightful vein in those points of highest knowledge which before them lay hid to the world. For that wise Solon was directly a poet it is manifest, having written in verse the notable fable of the Atlantic Island which was continued by [fifth-century B.C. Greek philosopher] Plato [who wrote his philosophy in dialogue form borrowed from poetry]. And truly even Plato whosoever well considereth, shall find that in the body of his work, though the inside and strength were philosophy, the skin, as it were, and beauty depended most of poetry. For all standeth upon dialogues; wherein he feigneth many honest burgesses of Athens to speak of such matters that, if they had been set on the rack, they would never have confessed them; besides his poetical describing the circumstances of their meetings, as the well-ordering of a banquet, the delicacy of a walk, with interlacing mere tales, as Gyges' [a character in a story of magic told in Plato's *Republic*] Ring and others, which who knoweth not to be flowers of poetry did never walk into Apollo's garden.

And even historiographers, (although their lips sound of things done, and verity be written in their foreheads,) have been glad to borrow both fashion and perchance weight of poets. So [fifth-century B.C. Greek historian] Herodotus entituled his history by the name of the nine Muses; and both he and all the rest that followed him either stole or usurped of poetry their passionate describing of passions, the many particularities of battles which no man could affirm, or, if that be denied me, long orations put in the mouths of great kings and captains, which it is certain they never pronounced.

So that truly neither philosopher nor historiographer could, at the first, have entered into the gates of popular judgments, if they had not taken a great passport of poetry; which in all nations at this day, where learning flourisheth not, is plain to be seen, in all which they have some feeling of poetry. In Turkey, besides their lawgiving divines they have no other writers but poets. In our neighbour-country Ireland, where truly learning goeth very bare, yet are their poets held in a devout reverence. Even among the most barbarous and simple Indians, where no writing is, yet have they their poets, who make and sing songs (which they call *areytos* [a dance accompanied by song]), both of their ancestors' deeds and praises of their gods. A sufficient probability that, if ever learning come among them, it must be by having their hard dull wits softened and sharpened with the sweet delights of poetry; for until they find a pleasure in the exercises of the mind, great promises of much knowledge will little persuade them that know not the fruits of knowledge. In Wales, the true remnant of the ancient Britons, as there are good authorities to show the long time they had poets, which they called bards, so through all the conquests of Romans, Saxons, Danes, and Normans, some of whom did seek to ruin all memory of learning from among them, yet do their poets even to this day last; so as it is not more notable in soon beginning, than in long continuing.

The Poet as Holy Prophet

But since the authors of most of our sciences were the Romans, and before them the Greeks, let us a little stand upon their authorities, but even so far as to see what names they have given unto this now scorned skill. Among the Romans a poet was called *vates,* which is as much as a diviner, foreseer, or prophet, as by his conjoined words, *vaticinium* and *vaticinari,* is manifest; so heavenly a title did that excellent people bestow upon this heart-ravishing knowledge. And so far were they carried into the admiration thereof, that they thought in the chanceable hitting upon any such verses great foretokens of their following fortunes were placed; whereupon grew the word of *Sortes Virgilianae,* when by sudden opening Virgil's book they lighted upon any verse of his making; whereof the Histories of the Emperors' Lives are full: as of Albinus, the governor of our island, who in his childhood met with this verse,

> Arma amens capio, nec sat rationis in armis, [Distracted, I seize my arms, nor have I sufficient purpose in arms. Virgil, *Aeneid,* ii. 314.]

and in his age performed it; which although it were a very vain and godless superstition, as also it was to think that spirits were commanded by such verses—whereupon this word charms, derived of *carmina,* cometh [from the Latin *Carmen,* meaning chant or enchantment; chants were used in religious ceremonies to induce a hypnotic state] so yet serveth it to show the great reverence those wits were held in, and altogether not without ground, since both the oracles of Delphos and Sibylla's prophecies were wholly delivered in verses; for that same exquisite observing of number and measure in words, and that high-flying liberty of conceit [imagination] proper to the poet, did seem to have some divine force in it.

And may not I presume a little further to show the reasonableness of this word *vates,* and say that the holy David's Psalms are a divine poem? If I do, I shall not do it without the testimony of great learned men, both ancient and modern. But even the name Psalms will speak for me, which, being interpreted, is nothing but Songs; then, that it is fully written in metre, as all learned Hebricians agree, although the rules be not yet fully found; lastly and principally, his handling his prophecy, which is merely poetical. For what else is the awaking his musical instruments, the often and free changing of persons, his notable *prosopopoeias* [a poetic image attributing human form to that which is spiritual or inanimate], when he maketh you, as it were, see God coming in His majesty, his telling of the beasts' joyfulness and hills' leaping, but a heavenly poesy, wherein almost he showeth himself a passionate lover of that unspeakable and everlasting beauty to be seen by the eyes of the mind, only cleared by faith? But truly, now, having named him, I fear me I seem to profane that holy name, applying it to poetry, which is among us thrown down to so ridiculous an estimation. But they that with quiet judgments will look a little deeper into it, shall find the end and working of it such as, being rightly applied, deserveth not to be scourged out of the church of God.

But now let us see how the Greeks named it and how they deemed of it. The Greeks called him a Poet, which name hath, as the most excellent, gone through other languages. It cometh of this word *polein,* which is "to make"; wherein I know not whether by luck or wisdom we Englishmen have met with the Greeks in calling him a maker. Which name, how high and incomparable a title it is, I had rather were known by marking the scope of other sciences than by my partial allegation.

Bringing Forth a Better Nature

There is no art delivered unto mankind that hath not the works of nature for his principal object, without which they could not consist, and on which they so depend as they become actors and players, as it were, of what nature will have set forth. So doth the astronomer look upon the stars, and, by that he seeth, set down what order nature hath taken therein. So do the geometrician and arithmetician in their divers sorts of quantities. So doth the musician in times tell you which by nature agree, which not. The natural philosopher thereon hath his name, and the moral philosopher standeth upon the natural virtues, vices, and passions of man; and "follow nature," saith he, "therein, and thou shalt not err." The lawyer saith what men have determined; the historian what men have done. The grammarian speaketh only of the rules of speech, and the rhetorician and logician, considering what in nature will soonest prove and persuade, thereon give artificial rules, which still are compassed within the circle of a question, according to the proposed matter. The physician weigheth the nature of man's body, and the nature of things helpful or hurtful unto it. And the metaphysic [metaphysician, one who studies the philosophy of being and knowing], though it be in the second and abstract notions, and therefore be counted supernatural, yet doth he, indeed, build upon the depth of nature.

Only the poet, disdaining to be tied to any such subjection, lifted up with the vigour of his own invention, doth grow, in effect, into another nature, in making things either better than nature bringeth forth, or, quite anew, forms such as never were in nature, as the heroes, demi-gods, cyclops, chimeras, furies, and such like; so as he goeth hand in hand with Nature, not enclosed within the narrow warrant of her gifts, but freely ranging only within the zodiac [within the appointed heavenly path] of his own wit. Nature never set forth the earth in so rich tapestry as divers poets have done; neither with pleasant rivers, fruitful trees, sweet-smelling flowers, nor whatsoever else may make the too-much-loved earth more lovely; her world is brazen, the poets only deliver a golden.

Chapter 6

Daily Life

Chapter Preface

The Renaissance's emphasis on enjoyment of this life and de-emphasis on the afterlife found its initial expressions in art, politics, literature, science, and religion. But eventually, these principles were translated into details of the daily lives of the average person—some for better, others for worse.

A major casualty of the Renaissance ideals was feudalism, the medieval institution in which monarchs granted nobles land in exchange for their political loyalty, particularly in battle. The nobles in turn granted peasants the right to live on and work the land in exchange for payments of goods and money. The severe hardships of the peasants' daily life, for which they saw little return, made them less appreciative of the church's teachings to accept earthly burdens as the price of admittance into heaven. This was especially true in light of the vast amount of corruption they witnessed in the church. Many embraced the humanist philosophy of Protestantism, which placed each person's salvation in his or her own hands, rather than through those of a priest. This belief in self-determination inspired peasant uprisings and revolts that eventually led to higher wages and ownership of their own lands.

While the lot of the peasants improved, nobles in general did not fare as well. Their ranks shrank considerably as the cost of maintaining their castles and lands rose prohibitively. In addition, the introduction of gunpowder from Asia allowed monarchs to raise their own armies more cheaply. Now that gunpowder made even a peasant as formidable as the highly trained nobles, monarchs no longer had to risk having powerful nobles around who might band together and threaten his throne. Without royal support, many nobles were forced to sell their lands and join the royal army.

The greatest beneficiary of the Renaissance ideals was the

middle class, whose once limited horizons were considerably broadened. A robust economy helped create a prosperous middle class of merchants, traders, and bankers who sponsored art and built magnificent buildings. Conducting business required education, and as the merchant class became more educated, medieval beliefs about social class were cast aside. No longer were people limited to professions because of the class they were born into; many were now free to pursue careers based on their own talents and ambitions. As they did so and took their place in the new Renaissance society, they embraced self-help books, such as Leon Alberti's (1404–1472) *Four Books on the Family* and Baldassare Castiglione's (1478–1529) *Book of the Courtier,* which instructed educated people on how to behave properly in this new era.

The Courtier

Baldassare Castiglione

The qualities that defined the proper Renaissance gentleman and gentlewoman were thoroughly described in the widely popular *Il Cortegiano* (*The Courtier*) by Italian Baldassare Castiglione (1478–1529). Castiglione, who served as both a diplomat and a military leader, was himself a courtier, meaning one who regularly attends the royal court. Although written between 1513 and 1518, *The Courtier* wasn't published until 1528. Written in the dialogue form, the book serves as a manual for acceptable thinking and behavior for the courtier and the noble lady. For Castiglione, the courtier embodied the following qualities: be born an aristocrat, excel as a soldier, scholar, poet, athlete, and musician, and speak the elegant courtly language rather than the course dialect of the common people. In the book, Castiglione claims to report a lively discussion among a group of well-respected and witty nobles including Emilia Pia (d. 1528), Pietro Bembo (1470–1547), Count Ludovico da Canossa (1476–1532), and Costanza Fregosa.

The Courtier's popularity spread outside of Italy as it was translated into many languages. The English version was published in 1561, thirty-two years after Castiglione's death, where it became one of the most influential works of its day. English courtier Sir Philip Sidney claimed that he never traveled abroad without a copy in his pocket. Castiglione's own significance can be measured by the fact that his portrait, which hangs in France's famed Louvre museum, was painted by one of the great masters of Renaissance art, Raphael (1483–1520).

Excerpted from *The Book of the Courtier*, by Count Baldassare Castiglione, translated by Leonard Eckstein Opdycke (New York: Horace Liveright, 1901).

You [sixteenth-century Italian courtier Alfonso Ariosto] ask me then to write what is to my thinking the form of Courtiership most befitting a gentleman who lives at the court of princes, by which he may have the ability and knowledge perfectly to serve them in every reasonable thing, winning from them favour, and praise from other men, in short, what manner of man he ought to be who may deserve to be called a perfect Courtier without flaw. Wherefore, considering your request, I say that had it not seemed to me more blameworthy to be reputed somewhat unamiable by you than too conceited by everyone else, I should have avoided this task, for fear of being held over bold by all who know how hard a thing it is, from among such a variety of customs as are in use at the courts of Christendom, to choose the perfect form and as it were the flower of Courtiership. For custom often makes the same thing pleasing and displeasing to us; whence it sometimes follows that customs, habits, ceremonies and fashions that once were prized, become vulgar, and contrariwise the vulgar become prized. Thus it is clearly seen that use rather than reason has power to introduce new things among us, and to do away with the old; and he will often err who seeks to determine which are perfect. Therefore being conscious of this and many other difficulties in the subject set before me to write of, I am constrained to offer some apology, and to testify that this error (if error it may indeed be called) is common to us both, to the end that if I be blamed for it, the blame may be shared by you also; for your offence in setting me a task beyond my powers should not be deemed less than mine in having accepted it.

So now let us make a beginning of our subject, and if possible let us form such a Courtier that any prince worthy to be served by him, although of but small estate, might still be called a very great lord. . . .

True Grace

[Count Ludovico speaks:] "Beautiful teeth are very charming in a woman, for since they are not so much in view as the face is, but lie hidden most of the time, we may believe that less care is taken to make them beautiful than with the face. Yet if one were to laugh without cause and solely to display the teeth, he would betray his art, and however beautiful they were, would seem most ungraceful to all, like [first-century B.C. Roman poet Gaius Valerius] Catullus's Egnatius [character in Catullus's 39th ode]. It is the same with the hands; which, if they are delicate and beautiful, and occasionally left bare when there is need to use them, and not in order to display their beauty, they leave a very great desire to see more of them, and especially if covered with gloves again; for whoever covers them seems to have little care or thought whether they be seen or not, and to have them thus beautiful more by nature than by any effort or pains. . . .

A Courtier's Moral Qualities

"In this way we avoid and hide affectation, and you can now see how opposed and destructive it is to grace in every office as well of the body as the mind: whereof we have thus far spoken little, and yet we must not omit it, for since the mind is of far more worth than the body, it deserves to be more cultivated and adorned. And as to what ought to be done in the case of our Courtier, we will lay aside the precepts of the many sage philosophers who write of this matter and define the properties of the mind and discuss so subtly about their rank,—and keeping to our subject, we will in a few words declare it to be enough that he be (as we say) an honest and upright man; for in this are included prudence, goodness, strength and temperance of mind, and all the other qualities that are proper to a name so honoured. And I esteem him alone to be a true moral philosopher, who wishes to be good; and in this regard he needs few other precepts than that wish. And therefore [fifth-century B.C. Greek philosopher] Socrates was right in saying that he thought his teachings bore good fruit indeed whenever they incited anyone to understand and teach virtue: for they who have reached the goal of desiring nothing more ardently than to be good, easily acquire knowledge of everything needful therefor; so we will discuss this no further.

The Importance of Learning

"Yet besides goodness, I think that letters are for everyone the true and principal ornament of the mind: although the French recognize only the nobility of arms and esteem all else as naught. Thus they not only fail to prize but they abhor letters, and hold all men of letters most base, and think they speak very basely of any man when they call him a clerk."

Then the Magnifico Giuliano replied:

"You say truly, that this fault has long been prevalent among the French. But if kind fate decrees that Monseigneur d'Angoulême shall succeed to the crown, as is hoped, I think that just as the glory of arms flourishes and shines in France, so too ought that of letters to flourish in highest state; for it is not long since I, being at the court, saw this prince, and it seemed to me that besides the grace of his person and the beauty of his face, he had in his aspect such loftiness, joined however with a certain gracious humanity, that the realm of France must always seem small for him. I heard afterwards from many gentlemen, both French and Italian, of his very noble manner of life, of his loftiness of mind, of his valour and liberality. And among other things I was told that he loved and esteemed letters especially and held all men of letters in greatest honour; and he condemned the French themselves for being so hostile to this profession, especially as they have within their borders such a noble school as that of Paris, frequented by all the world."

Then the Count said:

"It is a great marvel that in such tender youth, solely by natural instinct and against the usage of his country, he has of himself chosen so worthy a path. And as subjects always copy the customs of their superiors, it may be that, as you say, the French will yet come to esteem letters at their true worth: whereto they may easily be persuaded, if they will but listen to reason; since nothing is by nature more desirable for men, or more proper to them, than knowledge, which it is great folly to say or believe is not always a good thing.

"And if I were speaking with them, or with others who had an opinion contrary to mine, I should strive to show them how useful and necessary letters are to our life and dignity, having indeed been granted by God to men as a crowning gift. Nor should I lack instances of many excellent commanders of antiquity, who all added the ornament of letters to the valour of their arms. . . .

Mature Love Is Rational

Bembo still sought to put an end to his discourse, but my lady Duchess begged him to speak; and he began anew thus:

"Too unhappy would human nature be, if our soul (wherein such ardent desire can spring up easily) were forced to feed it solely upon that which is common to her with the beasts, and could not direct it to that other nobler part which is peculiar to herself. Therefore, since so indeed it pleases you, I have no wish to avoid discoursing upon this noble subject. And as I feel myself unworthy to speak of Love's most sacred mysteries, I pray him so to inspire my thought and tongue that I may be able to show this excellent Courtier how to love beyond the manner of the vulgar crowd; and since from boyhood up I have dedicated my whole life to him, so now also may my words comport with this intent and with his praise.

"I say, then, that as in youth human nature is so greatly prone to sense, the Courtier may be allowed to love sensually while he is young. But if afterwards in maturer years he chances still to be kindled with this amorous desire, he must be very wary and take care not to deceive himself by allowing himself to be led into those calamities which in the young merit more compassion than blame, and, on the contrary, in the old more blame than compassion.

"Therefore when the gracious aspect of some fair woman meets his view, accompanied with such sweet behaviour and gentle manners that he, as an adept in love, feels that his spirit accords with hers: as soon as he finds that his eyes lay hold upon her image and carry it to his heart; and that his soul begins to contemplate her with pleasure and to feel that influence within which stirs and warms it little by little; and that those quick spirits which shine out through the eyes continually add fresh tinder to the fire;—he ought at this first stage to provide a speedy cure, and arouse his reason, and therewith arm the fortress of his heart, and so shut the way to sense and appetite that they cannot enter there by force or trickery. Thus, if the flame is extinguished, the danger is extinguished also; but if it survives or grows, then the Courtier, feeling himself caught, must resolve on shunning wholly every stain of vulgar love, and thus enter on the path of divine love, with reason for guide. And first he must consider that the body wherein this beauty shines is not the fountain whence it springs, but rather that beauty (being an incorporeal thing and, as we have said, a heavenly beam) loses much of its dignity when it finds itself joined to vile and corruptible matter; for the more perfect it is the less it partakes thereof, and is most perfect when wholly separate therefrom. And he must consider that just as one cannot hear with the palate or smell with the ears, so too can beauty in no wise be enjoyed, nor can the desire which it excites in our minds be satisfied, by means of touch, but by that sense of which this beauty is the very object, namely, the power of vision.

"Therefore let him shun the blind judgment of sense, and with his eyes enjoy the splendour of his lady, her grace, her amorous sparkle, the laughs, the ways and all the other pleasant ornaments of her beauty. Likewise with his hearing let him enjoy the sweetness of her voice, the concord of her words, the harmony of her music (if this beloved be a musician). Thus will he feed his soul on sweetest food by means of these two senses—which have little of the corporeal and are ministers of reason—without passing in his desire for the body to any appetite less than seemly.

"Next let him obey, please and honour his lady with all reverence, and hold her dearer than himself, and prefer her convenience and pleasures to his own, and love in her not less the beauty of mind than that of body. Therefore let him take care not to leave her to fall into any kind of error, but by admonition and good advice let him always seek to lead her on to modesty, to temperance, to true chastity, and see to it that no thoughts find place in her except those that are pure and free from every stain of vice; and by thus sowing virtue in the garden of her fair mind, he will gather fruits of fairest behaviour too, and will taste them with wonderful delight. And this will be the true engendering and manifesting of beauty in beauty, which by some is said to be the end of love.

"In such fashion will our Courtier be most acceptable to his lady, and she will always show herself obedient, sweet and affable to him, and as desirous of pleasing him as of being loved by him; and the wishes of both will be most virtuous and harmonious, and they themselves will thus be very happy."

The Perfect Wife

Leon Battista Alberti

Italian Leon Battista Alberti (1404–1472) is often compared
to Leonardo da Vinci (1452–1519) in that he embodied so
many of the virtues of the Renaissance Man. He was a poet,
scholar, architect, mathematician, engineer, cartographer, and
theorist who wrote books on most of those disciplines. In
1432 he began the *Della famiglia* (*On the Family*), a book in
dialogue form that would offer the wisdom of ancient
philosophers to instruct his contemporary reader in the ways
of daily life, including advice on education, friendship, citi-
zenship, and family relations. To ensure the widest possible
audience, Alberti broke with the tradition of writing in Latin
and published his treatise in Tuscan, a dialect of Italian. To
Alberti, moral behavior arose out of virtuous action, not
merely good thoughts. The following excerpt from *On the
Family* outlines the proper behavior of a wife.

After my wife had been settled in my house a few days,
and after her first pangs of longing for her mother and
family had begun to fade, I took her by the hand and showed
her around the whole house. I explained that the loft was the
place for grain and that the stores of wine and wood were
kept in the cellar. I showed her where things needed for the
table were kept, and so on, through the whole house. At the
end there were no house-hold goods of which my wife had
not learned both the place and the purpose. Then we returned to my room, and, having locked the door, I showed
her my treasures, silver, tapestry, garments, jewels, and

Excerpted from "On the Family," by Leon Battista Alberti, *The Renaissance Reader*,
edited by Kenneth J. Atchity (New York: HarperPerennial, 1997).

where each thing had its place. . . .

Only my books and records and those of my ancestors did I determine to keep well sealed. . . . These my wife not only could not read, she could not even lay hands on them. I kept my records at all times . . . locked up and arranged in order in my study, almost like sacred and religious objects. I never gave my wife permission to enter that place, with me or alone. I also ordered her, if she ever came across any writing of mine, to give it over to my keeping at once. To take away any taste she might have for looking at my notes or prying into my private affairs, I often used to express my disapproval of bold and forward females who try too hard

A New Era for Women

The Renaissance encouraged debate about the nature of women and their role in society. Reason and logic were emphasized rather than just adhering to tradition for its own sake. Louise Labé (c. 1524–1566), renowned for her wit and charm, rose to fame as a poet during this time by expressing the qualities of the era. Born in Lyon, the first French hub of the Renaissance, she became known for her many accomplishments as well as her insistence on personal freedom. Her strong personality resulted in many legendary exploits being attributed to her, including that she rode into battle dressed as a man and spent time as a courtesan (a prostitute to members of the royal court). In 1555, Labé published a book of love sonnets known for their emotional intensity. The following excerpt from the "Preface, to a Friend," extols the virtues of education for women and the advantages to society of women being given equal opportunities as men.

Since a time has come, Mademoiselle, when the severe laws of men no longer prevent women from applying themselves to the sciences and other disciplines, it seems to me that those of us who can should use this long-craved freedom to study and to let men see how greatly they wronged us when depriving us of its honor and advantages. And if any to know about things outside the house and about the concerns of their husband and of men in general. . . .

[Husbands] who take counsel with their wives . . . are madmen if they think true prudence or good counsel lies in the female brain. . . . For this very reason I have always tried carefully not to let any secret of mine be known to a woman. I did not doubt that my wife was most loving, and more discreet and modest in her ways than any, but I still considered it safer to have her unable, and not merely unwilling, to harm me. . . . Furthermore, I made it a rule never to speak with her of anything but household matters or questions of conduct, or of the children. Of these matters I spoke a good deal to her. . . .

woman becomes so proficient as to be able to write down her thoughts, let her do so and not despise the honor but rather flaunt it instead of fine clothes, necklaces, and rings. For these may be considered ours only by use, whereas the honor of being educated is ours entirely. . . . If the heavens had endowed me with sufficient wit to understand all I would have liked, I would serve in this as an example rather than an admonishment. But having devoted part of my youth to musical exercises, and finding the time left too short for the crudeness of my understanding, I am unable, in my own case, to achieve what I want for our sex, which is to see it outstrip men not only in beauty but in learning and virtue. All I can do is to beg our virtuous ladies to raise their minds somewhat above their distaffs and spindles and try to prove to the world that if we were not made to command, still we should not be disdained as companions in domestic and public matters by those who govern and command obedience. Apart from the good name that our sex will acquire thereby, we shall have caused men to devote more time and effort in the public good to virtuous studies for fear of seeing themselves left behind by those over whom they have always claimed superiority in practically everything.

Julia O'Faolain and Lauro Martines, eds., *Not in God's Image*. New York: Harper & Row, 1973.

When my wife had seen and understood the place of everything in the house, I said to her, 'My dear wife . . . you have seen our treasures now, and thanks be to God they are such that we ought to be contented with them. If we know how to preserve them, these things will serve you and me and our children. It is up to you, therefore, my dear wife, to keep no less careful watch over them than I.'

A Wife's Duties

. . . She said she would be happy to do conscientiously whatever she knew how to do and had the skill to do, hoping it might please me. To this I said, 'Dear wife, listen to me. I shall be most pleased if you do just three things: first, my wife, see that you never want another man to share this bed but me. You understand.' She blushed and cast down her eyes. Still I repeated that she should never receive anyone into that room but myself. That was the first point. The second, I said, was that she should take care of the household, preside over it with modesty, serenity, tranquility, and peace. That was the second point. The third thing, I said, was that she should see that nothing went wrong in the house.

[Addressing the other interlocutors] . . . I could not describe to you how reverently she replied to me. She said her mother had taught her only how to spin and sew, and how to be virtuous and obedient. Now she would gladly learn from me how to rule the family and whatever I might wish to teach her.

. . . Then she and I knelt down and prayed to God to give us the power to make good use of those possessions which he, in his mercy and kindness, had allowed us to enjoy. We also prayed . . . that he might grant us the grace to live together in peace and harmony for many happy years, and with many male children, and that he might grant to me riches, friendship, and honor, and to her, integrity, purity, and the character of a perfect mistress of the household. Then, when we had stood up, I said to her: 'My dear wife, to have prayed God for these things is not enough. . . . I shall seek with all my powers to gain what we have asked of God. You, too, must set your whole will, all your mind, and all your modesty to work to make yourself a person whom God has heard. . . . You should realize that in this regard nothing is so important for yourself, so acceptable to God, so pleasing to me, and precious in the sight of your children as your chastity. The woman's character is the jewel of her family; the mother's purity has always been a part of the dowry she passes on to her daughters; her purity has always far out-weighed her beauty. . . . Shun every sort of dishonor, my dear wife. Use every means to appear to all people as a highly respectable woman. To seem less would be to offend God, me, our children, and yourself.'

[Finally, turning to the interlocutors again] . . . Never, at any moment, did I choose to show in word or action even the least bit of self-surrender in front of my wife. I did not imagine for a moment that I could hope to win obedience from one to whom I had confessed myself a slave. Always, therefore, I showed myself virile and a real man.

The Judgment of a Witch

Fugger News-Letter

Accusations of witchcraft were deadly serious during the Middle Ages and the Renaissance because a conviction could lead to torture and even death. Hundreds of thousands of women were executed as witches during this time. The reasons for the rise of witchhunts during the otherwise enlightened Renaissance era are numerous. In part, there was a backlash against women making advances in education. In addition, religious leaders feared that the new scientific discoveries, especially the conclusion that the Earth was not the center of the universe, would result in people defying religion. Many people were convinced that the rise of religious and civil wars after 1500 foreshadowed a growing chaos that threatened to destroy society. Out of that fear came the rise of trials for witchcraft.

The following description of one such trial in 1587 was carried in the *Fugger News-Letter,* one of the earliest forerunners of the modern newspaper. The newsletter, circulated between 1572 and 1600, was used by the powerful Fugger family, a German banking and mercantile dynasty, to keep their many business concerns updated on the latest developments in European politics, religion, and arts so that they might gauge the impact these events would have on business.

The herein mentioned, malefic and miserable woman, Walpurga Hausmännin, now imprisoned and in chains,

Excerpted from "The Judgment of a Witch," by *Fugger News-Letter, The Portable Renaissance Reader,* edited by James Bruce Ross and Mary McLaughlin (New York: Viking Press, 1966).

has, upon kindly questioning and also torture, following on persistent and fully justified accusations, confessed her witchcraft and admitted the following. When one-and-thirty years ago she had become a widow, she cut corn for Hans Schlumperger, of this place, together with his former servant, Bis im Pfarrhof by name. Him she enticed with lewd speeches and gestures, and they convened that they should, on an appointed night, meet in her, Walpurga's, dwelling, there to indulge in lustful intercourse. So when Walpurga in expectation of this sat awaiting him at night in her chamber, meditating upon evil and fleshly thoughts, it was not the said bondsman who appeared unto her, but the Evil One in the latter's guise and raiment and indulged in fornication with her. Thereupon he presented her with a piece of money, in the semblance of half a thaler, but no one could take it from her, for it was a bad coin and like lead. For this reason she had thrown it away. After the act of fornication she saw and felt the cloven foot of her whoremonger, and that his hand was not natural, but as if made of wood. She was greatly affrighted thereat and called upon the name of Jesus, whereupon the Devil left her and vanished.

Selling Her Soul

On the ensuing night the Evil Spirit visited her again in the same shape and whored with her. He made her many promises to help her in her poverty and need, wherefore she surrendered herself to him body and soul. Thereafter the Evil One inflicted upon her a scratch below the left shoulder, demanding that she should sell her soul to him with the blood that had flowed therefrom. To this end he gave her a quill and, whereas she could not write, the Evil One guided her hand. She believes that nothing offensive was written, for the Evil One only swept with her hand across the paper. The script the Devil took with him, and whenever she piously thought of God Almighty, or wished to go to church, the Devil reminded her of it.

Further, the above-mentioned Walpurga confesses that she oft and much rode on a pitchfork by night with her paramour, but not far, on account of her duties. At such devilish trysts she met a big man with a grey beard, who sat in a chair, like a great prince, and was richly attired. That was the Great Devil to whom she had once more dedicated and promised herself body and soul. Him she worshipped and before him she knelt, and unto him she rendered other such-like honours. But she pretends not to know with what words and in which fashion she prayed. She only knows that once she heedlessly pronounced the name of Jesus. Then the above-mentioned Great Devil struck her in the face and Walpurga had to disown (which is terrible to relate) God in heaven, the Christian name and belief, the blessed saints and the holy Sacraments, also to renounce the heavenly hosts and the whole of Christendom. Thereupon the Great Devil baptized her afresh, naming her Höfelin, but her paramour-devil, Federlin. . . .

Loathsome Blasphemies

Since her surrender to the Devil, she had seemingly oft received the Blessed Sacrament of the true Body and Blood of Jesus Christ, apparently by the mouth, but had not partaken of it, but (which once more is terrible to relate) had always taken it out of her mouth again and delivered it up to Federlin, her paramour. At their nightly gatherings she had oft with her other playfellows trodden underfoot the Holy and Blessed Sacrament and the image of the Holy Cross. The said Walpurga states that during such-like frightful and loathsome blasphemies she at times truly did espy drops of blood upon the said Holy Sacrament, whereat she herself was greatly horrified. . . . She confesses, also, that her paramour gave her a salve in a little box with which to injure people and animals, and even the precious fruit of the field. He also compelled her to do away with and to kill young infants at birth, even before they had been taken to Holy Baptism. This she did, whenever possible. . . .

She rubbed with her salve and brought about the death of Lienhart Geilen's three cows, of Bruchbauer's horse, two years ago of Max Petzel's cow, three years ago of Duri

Striegel's cow, two years ago of Hans Striegel's cow, of the cow of the governor's wife, of a cow of Frau Schötterin, and two years ago of a cow of Michel Klingler, on the village green. In short, she confesses that she destroyed a large number of cattle over and above this. A year ago she found bleached linen on the common and rubbed it with her salve, so that the pigs and geese ran over it and perished shortly thereafter. Walpurga confesses further that every year since she has sold herself to the Devil she has on St. Leonard's Day exhumed at least one or two innocent children. With her devil-paramour and other playfellows she has eaten these and used their hair and their little bones for witchcraft.

She was unable to exhume the other children she had slain at birth, although she attempted it, because they had been baptized before God.

She had used the said little bones to manufacture hail; this she was wont to do once or twice a year. Once this spring, from Siechenhausen, downwards across the fields. She likewise manufactured hail last Whitsun, and when she and others were accused of having held a witches' revel, she had actually held one near the upper gate by the garden of Peter Schmidt. At that time her playfellows began to quarrel and struck one another, because some wanted to cause it to hail over Dillingen Meadows, others below it. At last the hail was sent over the marsh towards Weissingen, doing great damage. She admits that she would have caused still more and greater evils and damage if the Almighty had not graciously prevented and turned them away.

The Verdict

After all this, the Judges and Jury of the Court of this Town of Dillingen, by virtue of the Imperial and Royal Prerogative and Rights of his Right Reverence, Herr Marquard, bishop of Augsburg, and provost of the Cathedral, our most gracious prince and lord, at last unanimously gave the verdict that the aforesaid Walpurga Hausmännin be punished and dispatched from life to death by burning at the stake as being a maleficent and well-known witch and sorceress, convicted according to the context of Common Law and the Criminal Code of the Emperor Charles V and the Holy Roman Empire. All her goods and chattels and estate left after her to go to the Treasury of our most high prince and lord. The aforesaid Walpurga to be led, seated on a cart, to which she is tied, to the place of her execution, and her body first to be torn five times with red-hot irons. The first time outside the town hall in the left breast and the right arm, the second time at the lower gate in the right breast, the third time at the mill brook outside the hospital gate in the left arm, the fourth time at the place of execution in the left hand. But since for nineteen years she was a licensed and pledged midwife of the city of Dillingen, yet has acted so vilely, her right hand with which she did such knavish tricks is to be cut off at the place of execution. Neither are her ashes after the burning to remain lying on the ground, but are thereafter to be carried to the nearest flowing water and thrown thereinto. Thus a venerable jury have entrusted the executioner of this city with the actual execution and all connected therewith.

The Great Fire of London

Samuel Pepys

Englishman Samuel Pepys (1633–1703) (pronounced
"peeps") rose from modest origins to become a leading political figure as well as the friend to nearly every great scholar of
his time, including mathematician Sir Isaac Newton
(1642–1727). He was the first secretary of the admiralty as
well as a member of Parliament. But his most enduring work
was the diary that he kept between the ages of seventeen and
thirty-six, after which his eyesight grew too poor to continue.
More than just a record of personal thoughts and activities, it
details daily life in London with a richness and insight that
had never been done before. But having the characteristic
Renaissance appetite for unflinching truth, he did not neglect
recording his own frailties, including his infidelities, vanity,
and pettiness. As such, his diary symbolized the Renaissance
man and woman's striving to achieve spiritual and social
greatness while acknowledging their human frailties.

In the diary are accounts of many of the greatest moments
in the city's history, including the Restoration (the return of
the monarchy after the civil war) and the advent of the
plague. One well-known excerpt describes the Great Fire of
London of September 2, 1666. Here Pepys relates how widespread the fire was and how helpless officials were in fighting
it. Eventually, the fire destroyed most of the civic buildings,
eighty-seven parish churches, and about thirteen thousand
houses.

Excerpted from *The Diary of Samuel Pepys*, by Samuel Pepys (New York: The Heritage
Press, 1942).

[2nd] (Lord's day). Some of our mayds sitting up late last night to get things ready against our feast to-day, Jane called us up about three in the morning, to tell us of a great fire they saw in the City. So I rose and slipped on my night-gowne, and went to her window, and thought it to be on the back-side of Marke-lane at the farthest; but, being un-used to such fires as followed, I thought it far enough off; and so went to bed again and to sleep. About seven rose again to dress myself, and there looked out at the window, and saw the fire not so much as it was and further off. So to my closett to set things to rights after yesterday's cleaning. By and by Jane comes and tells me that she hears that above 300 houses have been burned down to-night by the fire we saw, and that it is now burning down all Fish-street, by London Bridge. So I made myself ready presently, and walked to the Tower, and there got up upon one of the high places, Sir J. Robinson's little son going up with me; and there I did see the houses at that end of the bridge all on fire, and an in-finite great fire on this and the other side the end of the bridge; which, among other people, did trouble me for poor little Michell and our Sarah on the bridge. So down, with my heart full of trouble, to the Lieutenant of the Tower, who tells me that it begun this morning in the King's baker's house in Pudding-lane, and that it hath burned St. Magnus's Church and most part of Fish-street already. So I down to the water-side, and there got a boat and through bridge, and there saw a lamentable fire. Poor Michell's house, as far as the Old Swan, already burned that way, and the fire running further, that in a very little time it got as far as the Steele-yard, while I was there. Everybody endeavouring to remove their goods, and flinging into the river or bringing them into lighters [small, flat-bottomed boats] that lay off; poor people staying in their houses as long as till the very fire touched them, and then running into boats, or clambering from one pair of stairs by the water-side to another. And among other things, the poor pigeons, I perceive, were loth to leave their houses, but hovered about the windows and balconys till they were, some of them burned, their wings, and fell down.

Having staid, and in an hour's time seen the fire rage every way, and nobody, to my sight, endeavouring to quench it, but to remove their goods, and leave all to the fire, and having seen it get as far as the Steele-yard, and the wind mighty high and driving it into the City; and every thing, after so long a drought, proving combustible, even the very stones of churches, and among other things the poor steeple by which pretty Mrs.—lives, and whereof my old schoolfellow Elborough is parson, taken fire in the very top, and there burned till it fell down: I to White Hall (with a gentleman with me who desired to go off from the Tower, to see the fire, in my boat); to White Hall, and there up to the King's closett in the Chappell, where people come about me, and I did give them an account dismayed them all, and word was carried in to the King [Charles II].

The King Orders Houses Destroyed

So I was called for, and did tell the King and Duke of Yorke what I saw, and that unless his Majesty did command houses to be pulled down nothing could stop the fire. They seemed much troubled, and the King commanded me to go to my Lord Mayor [Sir Thomas Bludworth] from him, and command him to spare no houses, but to pull down before the fire every way. The Duke of York bid me tell him that if he would have any more soldiers he shall; and so did my Lord Arlington afterwards, as a great secret. Here meeting with Captain Cocke, I in his coach, which he lent me, and Creed with me to Paul's, and there walked along Watling-street, as well as I could, every creature coming away loaden with goods to save, and here and there sicke people carried away in beds. Extraordinary good goods carried in carts and on backs. At last met my Lord Mayor in Canningstreet, like a man spent, with a handkercher about his neck. To the King's message he cried, like a fainting woman, "Lord! what can I do? I am spent: people will not obey me. I have been pulling down houses; but the fire overtakes us faster than we can do it." That he needed no more soldiers; and that, for himself, he must go and refresh himself, having been up all night. So he left me, and I him, and walked home, seeing people all almost distracted, and no manner of means used to quench the fire. The houses, too, so very thick thereabouts, and full of matter for burning, as pitch and tarr, in Thames-street; and warehouses of oyle, and wines, and brandy, and other things. Here I saw Mr. Isaake Houblon, the handsome man, prettily dressed and dirty, at his door at Dowgate, receiving some of his brothers' things, whose houses were on fire; and, as he says, have been removed twice already; and he doubts (as it soon proved) that they must be in a little time removed from his house also, which was a sad consideration. And to see the churches all filling with goods by people who themselves should have been quietly there at this time. By this time it was about twelve o'clock; and so home, and there find my guests, which was Mr. Wood and his wife Barbary Sheldon, and also Mr. Moone: she mighty fine, and her husband, for aught I see, a likely man. But Mr. Moone's design and mine, which was to look over my closett and please him with the sight thereof, which he hath long desired, was wholly disappointed; for we were in great trouble and disturbance at this fire, not knowing what to think of it. However, we had an extraordinary good dinner, and as merry as at this time we could be. While at dinner Mrs. Batelier come to enquire after Mr. Woolfe and Stanes (who, it seems, are related to them), whose houses in Fish-street are all burned, and they in a sad condition. She would not stay in the fright.

A Walk Through the Burning City

Soon as dined, I and Moone away, and walked through the City, the streets full of nothing but people and horses and carts loaden with goods, ready to run over one another, and removing goods from one burned house to another. They now removing out of Canning-streete (which received goods in the morning) into Lumbard-streete, and further; and among others I now saw my little goldsmith, Stokes, receiving some friend's goods, whose house itself was burned the day after. We parted at Paul's; he home, and I to Paul's Wharf, where I had appointed a boat to attend me, and took in Mr. Carcasse and his brother, whom I met in the streete, and carried them below and above bridge to and again to see the fire, which was now got further, both below and above, and no likelihood of stopping it. Met with the King and Duke of York in their barge, and with them to Queenhithe, and there called Sir Richard Browne to them. Their order was only to pull down houses apace, and so below bridge at the water-side; but little was or could be done, the fire coming upon them so fast. Good hopes there was of stopping it at the Three Cranes above, and at Buttolph's Wharf below bridge, if care be used; but the wind carries it into the City, so as we know not by the water-side what it do there. River full of lighters and boats taking in goods, and good goods swimming in the water, and only I observed that hardly one lighter or boat in three that had the goods of a house in, but there was a pair of Virginalls [piano-like musical instrument] in it. Having seen as much as I could now, I away to White Hall by appointment, and there walked to St. James's Parke, and there met my wife and Creed and Wood and his wife, and walked to my boat; and there upon the water again, and to the fire up and down, it still encreasing, and the wind great. So near the fire as we could for smoke; and all over the Thames, with one's face in the wind, you were almost burned with a shower of fire-drops. This is very true; so as houses were burned by these drops and flakes of fire, three or four, nay, five or six houses, one from another. When we could endure no more upon the water, we to a little ale-house on the Bankside, over against the Three Cranes, and there staid till it was dark almost, and saw the fire grow; and, as it grew darker, appeared more and more, and in corners and upon steeples, and between churches and houses, as far as we could see up the hill of the City, in a most horrid malicious bloody flame, not like the fine flame of an ordinary fire. Barbary and her husband away before us.

The Fire Closes In

We staid till, it being darkish, we saw the fire as only one entire arch of fire from this to the other side the bridge, and in a bow up the hill for an arch of above a mile long: it made me weep to see it. The churches, houses, and all on fire and flaming at once; and a horrid noise the flames made, and the cracking of houses at their ruine. So home with a sad heart, and there find every body discoursing and lamenting the fire; and poor Tom Hater come with some few of his goods saved out of his house, which is burned upon Fish-streete Hill. I invited him to lie at my house, and did receive his goods, but was deceived in his lying there, the newes coming every moment of the growth of the fire; so as we were forced to begin to pack up our owne goods, and prepare for their removal; and did by moonshine (it being brave dry, and moonshine, and warm weather) carry much of my goods into the garden, and Mr. Hater and I did remove my money and iron chests into my cellar, as thinking that the safest place. And got my bags of gold into my office, ready to carry away, and my chief papers of accounts also there, and my tallys into a box by themselves. So great was our fear, as Sir W. Batten hath carts come out of the country to fetch away his goods this night. We did put Mr. Hater, poor man, to bed a little; but he got but very little rest, so much noise being in my house, taking down of goods.

Chronology

1353
Giovanni Boccaccio writes the *Decameron,* inventing the Italian novella.

1395
Earliest known English poet, Geoffrey Chaucer, publishes *Canterbury Tales.*

c. 1400
Renaissance begins in northern Italy; all of Europe is now Christian.

1414
The Medici family of bankers becomes the most powerful family in Florence, Italy, ruling it for several generations.

1430
Modern English develops from Middle English.

1431
After leading French troops against the English army in France during the Hundred Years' War (1337–1453), Joan of Arc (1412–1431) is captured and burned at the stake for heresy and witchcraft.

1450
Under the rule of the Medici family, patrons of some of the most illustrious artists and architects, Florence becomes the artistic center of the Renaissance.

1453

The Turks conquer Constantinople, ending the Eastern Roman (Byzantine) Empire; end of the Hundred Years' War between England and France.

1454

German goldsmith Johannes Gutenberg invents the printing press with movable type; the Gutenberg Bible is published.

1466

Johann Mentel prints the first Bible in German.

1467

William Caxton prints the first book in English.

1483

Pope Alexander VI divides the New World between Spain and Portugal.

1484

Roman Catholic Church declares the existence of witchcraft.

1492

Italian explorer Christopher Columbus lands on Watling Island, Bahamas, and claims the New World for Spain; Jews are given three months to convert to Christianity or be expelled from Spain.

1495

Jews are expelled from Portugal; French soldiers initiate a syphilis epidemic throughout Europe.

1495–1498

Italian artist Leonardo da Vinci paints *Last Supper.*

1497–1498

Portuguese navigator Vasco da Gama reaches India and Africa.

1499
Italian artist Michelangelo sculpts *Pieta*.

1500
The Portuguese claim Brazil and establish regular trade with India.

1501
The Spanish introduce African slaves to the West Indies; Portuguese explorer Amerigo Vespucci explores South America, which he calls "America."

1502
German locksmith Peter Henlein (1480–1542) makes the first watch, the "Nuremberg Egg."

1508
Michelangelo begins painting the Sistine Chapel in Rome.

1509
Roman Catholic bishop Bartolomé de las Casas suggests that each Spanish settler should take African slaves to the New World; Dutch priest and humanist scholar Desiderius Erasmus publishes *In Praise of Folly*, satirizing church corruption.

1512
Polish astronomer Nicolaus Copernicus publishes his observation that the earth rotates around the sun, despite commonly held belief that the reverse is true; Michelangelo completes the Sistine Chapel frescoes.

1513
Italian politician Niccolò Machiavelli publishes *The Prince*, a guide to teach monarchs how to rule ruthlessly.

1517
Portuguese explorer Ferdinand Magellan begins first voyage to circle the world; only one ship returns successfully, in 1522; German cleric Martin Luther posts his Ninety-Five Theses on the door of the Wittenberg church, heralding the founding of Protestantism.

1520
Chocolate brought from Mexico to Spain; Luther is excommunicated by the church.

1521
Luther argues for "justification by faith alone," marking the start of the Protestant Reformation.

1525
Luther translates the Bible into German.

1528
Italian courtier Baldassare Castiglione publishes *The Courtier,* a book of manners for upper-class courtiers.

1531
When the pope refuses to annul English monarch Henry VIII's marriage, he declares himself Supreme Head of the Church of England (Anglican Church).

1534
Spanish religious leader Ignatius Loyola founds the Jesuit order.

1542
The Portuguese become first Westerners to land in Japan.

1543
The Spanish Inquisition begins burning Protestants as heretics.

1550
The influx of silver from America to Spain encourages the rise of the middle class.

1555
Tobacco is brought to Spain from America for the first time.

1560
Puritanism begins in England; Scotland adopts Protestantism as national faith.

1562
English naval commander John Hawkins establishes slave trade between Africa and West Indies.

1565
Spanish establish colonies in Florida; tobacco from America is introduced into England as a powerful medicine.

1570
The potato is introduced to Europe from South America.

1577–1580
English explorer Sir Francis Drake circumnavigates the world.

1588
Spanish Armada is defeated, ending Spain's hopes of conquering England.

1591
English playwright William Shakespeare begins writing plays.

1592
The plague kills fifteen thousand people in London.

1596
Indoor bathrooms (water closets) are installed at Queen's Palace, Richmond, England; Italian astronomer Galileo Galilei invents the thermometer.

1605
Spanish writer Miguel de Cervantes publishes part one of Europe's first novel, *Don Quixote*; the second part is published in 1615.

1607
The first permanent English colony in America is founded at Jamestown, Virginia.

1608
Dutch scientist Johann Lippershey invents the telescope.

1610
Galileo discovers the moons of Jupiter and the phases of Venus.

1611
The King James Version of the Bible is published.

1612
The last recorded burning of heretics takes place in England.

1616
The church forbids Galileo from any further scientific work.

1618
The Thirty Years' War begins in Europe.

1619
The first black slaves in North America arrive in Virginia.

1620
Pilgrims land in New England; English scientist Sir Francis Bacon introduces the scientific method of experimentation and observation in *Novum Organum*.

1628
Englishman William Harvey describes the circulation of the blood in the human body.

1633
Inquisition forces Galileo to reject Copernicus's theories.

1636
Harvard College (later University) founded.

1637
French mathematician and philosopher René Descartes publishes *Discourse on Method*, ushering in the scientific age.

1639
First printing press in North America is established in Cambridge, Massachusetts.

1642
The English civil war begins (ends in 1649).

1643
Louis XIV, the last of the Renaissance dictators, begins reign (which ends in 1715).

1648
Due to famine, war, and plague, population of Germany shrinks from 17 million to 8 million; George Fox (1624–1691) founds the Society of Friends (Quakers).

1655

English ruler Oliver Cromwell dissolves Parliament, bans Anglican services, allows Jews to return to England.

1660

Monarchy is restored in England.

1665

English mathematician Isaac Newton experiments on gravity and invents differential calculus; Great Plague in London (July–October) kills 68,596 people.

For Further Research

Margaret Aston, ed., *The Panorama of the Renaissance*. New York: Harry N. Abrams, 1996.

Kenneth J. Atchity, ed., *The Renaissance Reader.* New York: HarperCollins, 1996.

Roland H. Bainton et al., *The Renaissance: Maker of Modern Man*. Washington, DC: National Geographic Society, 1970.

C. Black et al., *Renaissance.* Chicago: Stonehenge, 1993.

Fernand Braudel, *Capitalism and Material Life, 1400–1800*. New York: Harper & Row, 1973.

———, *A History of Civilizations.* New York: Penguin Press, 1994.

Jacob Burckhardt, *The Civilization of the Renaissance*. New York: Oxford University Press, 1945.

Peter Burke, *Culture and Society in Renaissance Italy, 1420–1540*. New York: Charles Scribner's Sons, 1972.

Ernst Cassirer et al., eds., *The Renaissance Philosophy of Man*. Chicago: University of Chicago Press, 1948.

E.R. Chamberlin, *Everyday Life in Renaissance Times*. London: B.T. Batsford, 1965.

Alison Cole, *Virtue and Magnificence: Art of the Italian Renaissance Courts*. New York: Harry N. Abrams, 1995.

Vincent Cronin, *The Florentine Renaissance*. London: Collins, 1967.

Marcel Dunan, ed., *Larousse Encyclopedia of Modern History: From 1500 to the Present Day*. New York: Harper & Row, 1964.

Will Durant, *The Renaissance: A History of Civilization in Italy from 1304–1576 A.D.* New York: Simon and Schuster, 1953.

Editors of Reader's Digest, *Everyday Life Through the Ages.* London: Reader's Digest, 1992.

Editors of Time-Life Books, *What Life Was Like at the Rebirth of Genius: Renaissance Italy A.D. 1400–1500.* Alexandria, VA: Time-Life Books, 1999.

J.H. Elliott, *The Old World and the New, 1492–1650.* Cambridge, England: Cambridge University Press, 1970.

Wallace Ferguson and Geoffrey Bruun, *A Survey of European Civilization,* 3rd ed. New York: Houghton Mifflin, 1962.

John Gage, *Life in Italy: At the Time of the Medici.* London: B.T. Batsford, 1968.

Paul F. Grendler, ed., *An Italian Renaissance Reader.* Toronto: University of Toronto Press, 1992.

J.R. Hale, *Renaissance Europe.* New York: Harper & Row, 1971.

Denys Hays, ed., *The Age of the Renaissance.* London: Thames and Hudson, 1986.

Lisa Jardine, *Worldly Goods: A New History of the Renaissance.* New York: Doubleday, 1996.

De Lamar Jensen, *Reformation Europe: Age of Reform and Revolution.* Lexington, MA: D.C. Heath, 1981.

Margaret King, *Women of the Renaissance.* Chicago: University of Chicago Press, 1991.

Christiane Klapisch-Zuber, *Women, Family, and Ritual in Renaissance Italy.* Trans. Lydia Cochrane. Chicago: University of Chicago Press, 1985.

Jill Kraye, ed., *The Cambridge Guide to Renaissance Humanism.* Cambridge, England: Cambridge University Press, 1998.

J. Lucas-Dubreton, *Daily Life in Florence: In the Time of the Medici.* Trans. A. Lytton Sells. New York: Macmillan, 1961.

Richard B. McBrien, *Lives of the Popes: The Pontiffs from St. Peter to John Paul II.* New York: HarperCollins, 1997.

I.D. McFarlane, *Renaissance France, 1470–1589*. New York: Barnes & Noble, 1974.

Charles L. Mee Jr., *Daily Life in the Renaissance*. New York: American Heritage, 1975.

John F.H. New, *The Renaissance and Reformation: A Short History*. New York: John Wiley & Sons, 1969.

John T. Paoletti and Gary M. Radke, *Art in Renaissance Italy*. Upper Saddle River, NJ: Prentice-Hall, 1997.

J.H. Plumb, *The Horizon Book of the Renaissance*. New York: American Heritage, 1961.

———, *Renaissance Profiles*. New York: Harper & Row, 1965.

James Bruce Ross and Mary Martin McLaughlin, *The Portable Renaissance Reader*. New York: Viking Press, 1966.

Richard C. Texler, *Public Life in Renaissance Florence*. New York: Academic Press, 1980.

Charles Van Doren, *A History of Knowledge*. New York: Ballantine, 1991.

Evelyn Welch, *Art and Society in Italy, 1350–1500*. Oxford: Oxford University Press, 1997.

Merry E. Wiesner, *Women and Gender in Early Modern Europe*. Cambridge, England: Cambridge University Press, 1993.

W.L. Wiley, *The Gentleman of Renaissance France*. Cambridge, MA: Harvard University Press, 1954.

Index